THE ACCIDENTAL ENTREPRENEUR

Practical Wisdom for People
Who Never Expected to Work for Themselves

Susan Urquhart-Brown

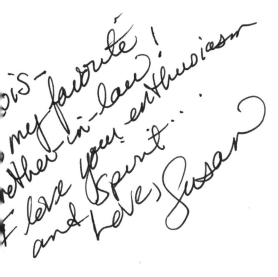

This book was designed to provide information on the subject matter covered. It is not the purpose of this manual to reprint all of the information available to the author/publisher, but to complement, amplify, and supplement other sources.

Use of *The Accidental Entrepreneur* does not in any way guarantee the success of an idea or an organization. When legal or other expert assistance is required, the services of a competent professional should be sought.

The author/publisher shall have neither liability nor responsibility to any person or entity with respect to any loss or damage caused, or alleged to be caused, directly or indirectly, by the information contained in this book.

Graphic Design and Illustrations: Coleen Patterson Design
Book Editor, Naomi Rose
Printed in the United States of America

Published by:

Career Steps
4112 Park Boulevard
Oakland, California 94602
www.careersteps123.com
510-531-2071

To Christopher, Christian, and Kevin Brown,

and my many friends and colleagues

who encouraged me along the way!

SPECIAL THANKS TO MY BOOK TEAM:

Jim Horan, Mentor,
One Page Business Plan Company

Naomi Rose, Book Editor,
Writing from the Deeper Self

Coleen Patterson,
Coleen Patterson Design

Don Landers III, Production,
Integrity by Design

Carol Anne Carroll, Proofreader,
Writing and Beyond

Masha Ovchinikov,
Word Processing and Proofreading

FOREWORD

by Jim Horan

Going solo is difficult . . . even for the best and strongest of entrepreneurs. The emotional ups and downs can be significant. In *The Accidental Entrepreneur*, Susan Urquhart-Brown speaks powerfully to the interpersonal aspects of self-employment as well as the practical nuts and bolts. Sometimes she offers a pep talk, encouraging you to try something new and bold. Other times, she gives a dose of "tough love" to get you back on track. But you always have a sense that the author is a real person who understands the people side of entrepreneurship, and that her advice is practical and real as well as inspiring.

One of the nice things about this book is that it is short, yet friendly. You can easily pick and choose which chapters to read and immediately apply what you learn to your business.

Who can benefit from reading this book? You can:

- If you are currently employed and considering starting a small business, *The Accidental Entrepreneur* will help you clearly decide whether self-employment is a good fit for you.

- If you do decide to venture forth and start a business, *The Accidental Entrepreneur* will help you here, too. The advice it gives is practical and proven. This is the best guidebook you could possibly buy.

- If you already own a small business and are ready to take it to the next level, the marketing and sales tips Susan shares in this book can really turbo-charge your business!

- If you are a professional coach, consultant or professor, you will want this book in your library – and it should be required reading for your clients or students, as well.

Unfortunately, far too many books on entrepreneurship are written by people who never started or built a business of their own. I've watched Susan build her business over the last ten years. This book shares not only what worked, but also what didn't. Both aspects are equally important.

I met Susan in about my third year of entrepreneurship. She coached me to develop workshops, encouraged me to write a best seller, urged me to add products to my consulting services, invited me to speak at world-class venues, and made countless numbers of incredibly important introductions. Thanks to Susan's advice (and an occasional kick in the butt), we have built The One Page Business Plan Company into a global "best practices company," complete with books, seminars, workshops and software.

Best wishes for building an incredibly successful business!

Jim Horan (another Accidental Entrepreneur)
President
The One Page Business Plan Company
Berkeley, California

TABLE OF CONTENTS

INTRODUCTION

What is an "accidental entrepreneur," anyway? The answer is: a person who never expected to be self-employed or thought of her/himself as an entrepreneur.

An accidental entrepreneur is not a born or natural entrepreneur, or even someone who is comfortable, at first, selling products or services. Accidental entrepreneurs don't set out to be entrepreneurs; rather, they find themselves working on their own by chance or reluctant choice, and only gradually come to find that they enjoy it. At that point, they realize that they need to learn what they don't already know – everything they can, in fact – in order to make their business a success.

Here are a few examples of accidental entrepreneurs:

- A communication specialist who takes a retirement package, and a few months later agrees to do a project for her former boss. The boss, enthused about the specialist's work, recommends her to someone in another company. Soon she is working on projects for three companies. One day it dawns on her that she has a consulting business. This is fine with her. But so far this work came strictly through referrals. How can she market herself to other companies?

- An engineer who has not been able to find work in the high-tech industry and needs money to pay his mortgage. He takes a substitute teaching job at a local school and discovers that many of his students need tutoring in math. He starts an after-school tutoring program and discovers that he really enjoys working with students, especially those who are math-phobic. He realizes that he could build a business around this. But how?

- A therapist, counselor, or coach who finds herself enjoying working one-on-one with clients and wants to build a private practice. She keeps her "day job" while slowly developing a referral base. At some point, she knows she wants to do this work full time, but she doesn't have enough clients to support herself to this degree. What steps does she need to take in order to accomplish this goal?

- A corporate refugee whose vision is to live a quieter life, away from the city, and manages to move with her husband to a small tourist town. However, this new area offers very few well-paying jobs. The couple realize that they need to make their living on their own, and decide to open a gift store, although neither of them has any retail experience. They decide to invest their savings in this store. What do they need to learn in order to make the store a moneymaker and to keep its doors open over time?

In all these cases, and many more like them, the decision to be an entrepreneur comes about gradually, as events change, priorities shift, and the need to make a living creates new needs and new possibilities. And, in almost every one of these cases, there's a lot to consider before just jumping in, if the business is to get off the ground and keep on going.

Passion and motivation are the first considerations. Entrepreneurship is like running a marathon. You might run to lose weight, to get in shape, to prove you can do it, or for a cause. These are all good reasons. But do they have sticking power? Is your heart really in it? Before you took your first running step, it would help to ask yourself, "Why am I doing this?" If your answer was, "Because I'm enthusiastic and passionate about it," then you would have a good chance. When your heart is truly connected with your goal, you are willing to train, to run, to move past your obstacles, reach the finish line, and celebrate your success – and then do it all over again! (The next time, however, you can learn from your mistakes and get to the finish line faster!)

You may begin your entrepreneurial career by accident, but it's important to make this *intentional* as soon as possible. For only once it becomes intentional will you give your business the kind of care it needs, and make it possible for it to give back to you the kind of profit and enjoyment you hoped for in the first place.

Being an entrepreneur is far more creative than doing a job for someone else. Your business is a reflection of who you are and what you're passionate about, as well as the unique expertise you have to offer the marketplace. If you are a sole proprietor – or, as I like to say, a "SoloPreneur" – *you* make all the decisions, *you* do most of the work, *you* solve the problems, *you* take the heat when things go wrong, and *you* bask in the glory when things go right. It's exciting and scary, but you are doing what you love.

How to Use This Book

I have a dream that everyone whose heart's desire is to have a successful business has the opportunity to manifest the business that best fits their expertise, passion, and the needs of their perfect clients or customers. This guidebook will boost your confidence and give you tools and techniques to reach your goals, one step at a time!

This book can be digested in bite-sized pieces. Look at the table of contents, then turn to the section that interests you most. Read one chapter. Do one exercise. Apply the ideas directly to your business. Read one whole section at one sitting. Prioritize the ideas, tools, or techniques that fit your business strategies and that you would like to implement. Then add them to your action-item list or business plan.

In other words, this guidebook is designed to be useful, practical, accessible, and encouraging . . . and, most of all, to guide you from being an accidental entrepreneur to being an intentional entrepreneur with a thriving business.

PART ONE:

What *Is* An Entrepreneur, Anyway?

CHAPTER 1:

8 Questions to Ask Before You Start a Business

Have you been thinking about starting a business? Are you confused about where to start and what to do?

If you answered yes, your next move is to answer the following questions for yourself. This will help you in two ways: (1) you will gain clarity that will help you find direction, and (2) the thinking and research you do as you answer these questions will also become your steps for starting your business. Don't be like 95% of wannabe entrepreneurs who think they have a great idea and jump into business without careful planning. Some people who follow this strategy are very successful; but if you look before you leap, your percentage for success will be much higher.

> **REMEMBER:**
> *Even though there are obstacles along the way a marathon always has a well-planned course to follow.*

1. **"Who am I?"** Starting and running a business is a lot like running a marathon. There will be highs and lows, and the prospect is both exciting and scary. To maximize your chances, analyze your strengths and weaknesses as well as your personal characteristics. For example, to be in business, you need determination, persistence, creativity, flexibility, and a steep learning curve. Will you be able to develop and strengthen these characteristics better by working alone, being in a partnership, or being at the helm of a fast-growing organization? How does your business idea fit in with your personal goals for the next 3-5 years? *Your business idea, your expertise, and your personality all need to fit well with the type of company you're growing.*

2. **"What business am I in?"** Carefully define and detail what your product and/or services are. What problems do you solve? What benefits do you provide? Who are you targeting to buy your services? Consumers? Organizations? Where are they located? How will you reach them? For example, if you want to build a coaching practice, what type of coaching do you offer – executive coaching in which your clients are corporations, or personal coaching in which your clients are individuals? *Learn everything you can about the business you want to start and the marketplace so that you know it inside and out.*

3. **"Is my business idea viable?"** In order to find out, market research is essential so that you can answer the questions: "Who will buy my product?" and "Are there enough potential customers out there for me to make a profit?" *Identify and analyze what your competitors are doing, and how what you offer is sufficiently different to attract customers.* But you don't need to do expensive focus groups. You can test market your idea with a group of friends and colleagues; interview competitors who are willing to talk to you; and research your industry and the market trends via the Internet or the local library. Other resources are the Small Business Administration Resource Centers, your local Chamber of Commerce, and successful entrepreneurs in a business related to yours.

4. **"What is my market niche?"** What is unique about you and your business? What do you want to be known for? If you fit your niche well, even in a recession, people will ask about your product or service first, and (the) price second. Hint: Having a niche does not mean offering the lowest price. Any competitor can charge less. *A market niche is what makes your business stand out from the pack. However, any old niche won't work. It has to be one that is focused, or*

narrow, but deep – that is, having enough potential customers in your targeted niche to bring you the business volume you want that will make your business profitable. For example, publishing companies are creating more specialty magazines. There is even one called *Prison Life*, which has a specialized but huge captive audience – literally.

5. **"How will I market my business?"** *The marketing strategies you choose must do two things: (1) reach your target customers, and (2) fit your business because you must continually market your business. Out of sight (or sound) is out of mind.* For example, speaking and writing is a good marketing mix for business consultants. Back-of-the-room sales are also brisk if you have authored a book. However, if you love to give talks but you own a retail store, your store location and a well-placed radio or TV/cable commercial might reach a wider audience of potential customers.

6. **"How will I finance my business?"** The flip side of the question, "Will I make enough money?" is "Do I have enough money to get started?" *Work with an accountant or business consultant to carefully determine how much start-up funding you need and help you do a profit-and-loss projection.* I recommend that you have enough personal funds to finance your living expenses for your first year of business. If you get a business loan, remember that you must put up collateral, which is often your house; if you get financing from angel investors, you must give up equity in your business, which means you won't have control over what your business really is and how you run it.

7. **"Why do I need a business plan?"** Now that you've decided to go into business and you have done your research, you are ready to write a business plan. *Planning ahead can mean the difference between success and failure.* This is the stage when you get your ideas out of your head and onto paper. You set your goals for the year, as well as strategies and specific plans for how you'll reach your goals. The written plan is a document that you can use to quickly explain your business to potential investors and – more importantly – to keep yourself on track.

8. **"Will I go into my own business?"** Are you going to run the marathon? Answering the above questions carefully will help you make a well-informed decision. If you're ready, start running now. *Remember: Even though there are obstacles along the way a marathon always has a well-planned course to follow.*

CHAPTER 2:

Myths About Going into Business for Yourself

Sometimes a person decides to go solo on a whim, based on some common myths about the joys of working for oneself. If you're considering starting a business, review the following common myths before you decide to proceed, so that you can avoid the pitfalls that go along with them.

There are many wonderful ideas and products that have never seen the light of day. It's much easier to come up with the ideas than to implement them.

- **Myth 1: "I'll try it out and see how it goes."** *Many people who are between jobs decide it's as good a time as any to start a business. However, choosing to go solo by default is not a wise idea.* Starting a business is very demanding and includes long working hours, financial investment, and, of course, no regular paycheck. It is not something to go into lightly. If all you are doing is "Trying It Out," it's bound to fail. Don't waste your time and money.

- **Myth 2: "When I'm my own boss, I'll avoid corporate politics."** *Experienced business owners know that they are not really their own boss. They have many more bosses than they ever did as an employee – bosses called "customers."* Some of their customers are corporations. So instead of dealing with the politics of a single company, you may have to handle the politics of 20. It's up to you to stay tuned into the needs and subtleties of each company and figure out how to meet those needs if you want to continue to be retained.

- **Myth 3: "I'll have more free time and flexible work hours."** *If you think you will have time to spend on your hobbies, play tennis a couple days a week, and schedule time off whenever you want, think again.* The first few years you will most likely spend 60 to 80 hours per week getting your business up and running. Moreover, the number of hours you spend working for yourself is not likely to lessen as your business grows. In addition to spending time delivering your service, you will be marketing your services, running your business, doing paperwork, solving problems, and developing new products and services. It's important to be realistic about how many hats you have to wear as a business owner and how much time it really takes to get everything done. One client of mine said," Yes, I have flexible hours. I can work until 2 a.m.!"

- **Myth 4: "All I need is a good idea."** *There are many wonderful ideas and products that have never seen the light of day. It's much easier to come up with the ideas than to implement them.* However, even if you follow through with building the better mousetrap, your business may not succeed. Even if you have a good idea and the technical expertise to create the product, you also need to be able to get others excited about the product and invest money in its production. You may need the services of an accountant, lawyer, banker, distributor, or vendor to make your product successful. All of these people need to buy into your idea or product. In short, you need not only a good idea, but also the ability to communicate your vision, a great business plan, and the ability to produce and sell the product with the help of your backers.

- **Myth 5: "After a few years, I'll make lots of money."** *Unless you are lucky or backed by venture capital, you probably won't get rich quick.* It takes 3 to 5 years to build a profitable, viable business. If you leave a corporate job to start your own business, this is a rule of thumb for income:

  - In the first year of business, you will make approximately 20% of your last salary.

  - By years 3 to 5, your profits can begin to grow substantially.

  You might be asking yourself, "If consultants make $1,000 to $3,000 a day, how can they *not* make a lot of money?" Because most consultants bill for services only about 55% of their time. The other 45% is spent on non-billable activities, such as accounting, marketing, planning, dealing with "administrivia" – everything else it takes to run a business. In your first year of business, you will spend a much higher percentage of your time on non-billable activities, such as marketing so that people know you exist.

If you're going to launch a business, it's best to have a dose of reality. Do your research and weigh all the factors carefully so that you can make an informed decision. Then, if the positives outweigh the negatives, by all means go for it!

CHAPTER 3:

Take the Entrepreneur Quiz!

Have you been downsized? Are you thinking about a career change? Are you taking early retirement? Have you said to yourself many times that you would start your own business if you only had a marketable idea? In the current economy, this may just be the time to develop a product or service and take the plunge into self-employment.

Even if you have never thought of yourself as an entrepreneur, you may already have the characteristics needed to become one. And even if you don't, you can develop them – *if* you are willing to take on the risks involved in being an entrepreneur as well as being motivated by the rewards.

The questions on the following page will help you determine whether you are ready to take the plunge into business ownership…

1. Are you comfortable with NOT receiving a regular paycheck?.....................YES ❑   NO ❑

2. Do you like work that offers challenge, change, and variety, even if it involves some risk? ....YES ❑   NO ❑

3. Are you flexible enough to meet changing market demands? ....YES ❑   NO ❑

4. Are you willing to invest your own money as well as ask others to invest in your business venture? ....YES ❑   NO ❑

5. Are you committed to spending as much time and effort as it takes to make your business successful? ....YES ❑   NO ❑

6. Is it important to you to do the strategic planning as well as take care of the day-to-day details of running a business?.....................YES ❑   NO ❑

7. Is your business idea based on your expertise, interests, and solid market research?..........YES ❑   NO ❑

8. Are you able to bounce back and learn from failures or temporary setbacks? ....YES ❑   NO ❑

9. Are you optimistic, persistent, and passionate about your work? ....YES ❑   NO ❑

10. Are you confident that you are capable of succeeding as an entrepreneur? ....YES ❑   NO ❑

Scoring the Quiz

8-10 Yeses: Ready to Move Ahead. If you answered Yes to 8-10 questions, you're ready to move into starting your own business. You are willing and able to take calculated risks supported by solid information and based on experience. You are probably energized by the work you do because it's stimulating and innovative and offers you opportunities to master challenges. You are an independent thinker who is willing to listen to the advice of others but you prefer to make your own decisions. *However, don't launch too fast.* Be sure to write your business plan, including a marketing plan and best-case/worst-case financials. Poor planning is still one of the most common reasons for business failure.

5-7 Yeses: Move Ahead Slowly. If you answered "Yes" to 5-7 questions, you have some of the key entrepreneurial characteristics, but you need to move ahead slowly. *Assess your strengths and weaknesses, and determine what you need to develop before you start a business.* You might consider buying a franchise or an existing business instead of starting a business from scratch. You might also test your mettle by starting your business part-time while working for someone else full- or part-time. Grow your business slowly, and only give up your employment when it grows large enough to be a viable business.

4-0 Yeses: Consider Working for Someone Else. *If you answered "Yes" to 4 or fewer of the questions, it's likely that you would be more comfortable working for someone else.* You're not sure of your ability to be your own boss and do what it takes to run a business. Perhaps you are interested in starting a business because you love delivering the service or making the product. If so, you might consider working for a company that values and fosters the entrepreneurial spirit, or join a start-up team within a larger company. *However, if you really* *want to start your own business, your determination can compensate for not having all of the entrepreneurial characteristics.* And of course, if you have a solid business idea, have evaluated the financial prospects carefully, have business partners you trust, and lots of capital, you might want to go for it.

Three Fear-Busters

No matter how you scored on this business "readiness" checklist, here are three things to keep in mind to help you get beyond the fear of taking the plunge into starting your own business.

1. *You don't have to start immediately.* It takes time to plan, and once you start your business it takes time to build it up. On average it takes between 3 and 5 years to build a solid, successful, profitable business. Make a plan, set your goals, and take one step at a time.

2. *Marketing and selling your product or service is much easier if you believe in yourself.* Base your business on your interests, strongest skills, and expertise.

3. *You don't need to do it all alone.* Get support from friends and family, advice from business professionals, business coaches, colleagues and take advantage of community resources. Don't fall into the trap of being the "lone wolf." This is a common mistake new entrepreneurs make. Ask for help when you need it – because, in the long run, you will save time and money!

PART TWO:

READY, SET, GO!

Chapter 4:

The Entrepreneurial Mystique

There's a mystique about the word "entrepreneur." People tend to say, "I'm not an entrepreneur. I'm a downsized executive who has a small consulting practice," or "I'm an independent contractor." I ask, "What's the difference?" Part of the mystique is thinking that the only *real* kind of entrepreneur is a person who has a brilliant idea and starts a business using venture capital, and the fledgling enterprise becomes the next Microsoft.

Not true. An entrepreneur is someone who organizes, manages, and assumes risk for a business or other enterprise, according to the Random House Dictionary. In other words, an entrepreneur is – or can be – you.

Choosing your own business fit is one of the most creative and difficult aspects of going solo.

Of course, some entrepreneurial ventures are more financially risky than others. If you are thinking about starting a business, you need to assess your level of comfort with risk, both financial and personal. Most people would try out their business schemes at least once if money were no object. However, it takes more than money to keep your venture growing and healthy. You need a passion for what you're doing, a persistent drive, and the confidence to keep up with marketplace trends.

What Type of Entrepreneurial Option Fits You Best?

The kind of entrepreneurial option you choose will have an effect on the risks you are willing to take. To determine what type of entrepreneurial option is best for you, assess your business vision versus how much risk you are willing to take.

Choosing your own business fit is one of the most creative and difficult aspects of going solo. In addition to thinking about whether your idea is marketable, consider what type of work reflects your passion and promises personal and professional fulfillment. Such a business will thrive because of your enthusiasm and commitment.

Here are two common approaches to becoming a SoloPreneur: (1) You want to be your own boss, but you don't have a clear idea of what business to start; and (2) You want to start a business based on your expertise, but you're afraid of the financial risk. However, if your business fits your unique skills, talents, and interests, and you have a solid plan, you can be successful either way.

Approach #1: You want to be your own boss, but don't know what business to start. Andrea was ready for a major life/work change. Knowing only that she wanted to be her own boss and live in the country, she quit her corporate job and moved to a small town in Northern California. Her business idea grew out of her frustration with being unable to find a good pair of shoes at local stores. She decided to fill the market void by opening a women's shoe store.

Although Andrea had no prior retail experience, she did have a background in corporate sales and marketing. She combined this savvy with the need for stylish women's shoes at affordable prices. After three years, her store was so successful that she sold it and opened a new store in another small town closer to her home in the country. Andrea did not start with a brand-new idea, but she did fill a market need that fit her skills and interests.

Approach #2: You want to start a business based on your expertise, but you're afraid of the financial risk. Carol was a single mom and a talented illustrator and graphic designer. She always wanted to be an artist, and had worked in the graphic design field for corporations and agencies since college. Over the years, Carol managed to do freelance projects after work and on weekends. But she was afraid to freelance full time, because she felt she needed to be very confident that her income would be the same (or increase) after going solo.

However, her freelance projects began multiplying to the point where she had no time to be with her family. After a year of almost around-the-clock work on the job and freelance projects on top of that, she went solo. It was a difficult and scary decision for her. Yet after one year on her own, Carol had more work than her old job and part-time freelance work had provided combined. And she loved working at home and creating designs that conveyed her customers' message colorfully, artistically, and effectively. What worked for Carol was careful planning and slowly building up a customer base in a field in which she already had expertise and contacts.

You Can Do It, Too

Both Carol and Andrea created successful businesses, even though sometimes they were scared and some of their friends thought they were crazy. *You can do it, too.* There are many resources and consultants to help you choose a good business fit. Surf the Internet, contact your local Chamber of Commerce or Small Business Administration, or browse through the small-business section of your local bookstore for ideas.

There is a myriad of information, from A to Z, detailing how to start a small business. Start planning, set goals, create your time line, and pick a starting date. Even the most confident entrepreneurs ask for help when they need it. My clients come to me, not just for a plan, but also to help keep them on track, maintain their focus, and build their business. That's why coaching is often part of a smart entrepreneur's plan – it gives perspective. An experienced third party can see your situation more clearly than you can, and offer useful guidance and encouragement on that basis.

CHAPTER 5:

Do You Have What It Takes?

Do you have what it takes to be a successful entrepreneur? As noted earlier, the dictionary defines an entrepreneur as "one who organizes, operates and especially assumes the risk of a business venture." [Random House Dictionary] The words that jump out from this definition are "assumes risk."

An essential element of entrepreneurship is taking calculated risks – not only when you start your business, but continually, as your business grows. Taking a calculated risk involves considering your options, knowing your business, and being ready to alter your direction when the market changes.

Some traits will fit you like a glove, while others will be a stretch – but all can be developed, even if you are an accidental entrepreneur.

One successful real estate entrepreneur I know says, "I don't see it as a risk. Once I've made up my mind to go for it, I have enough self-confidence and follow-through to make my project fly. From my point of view, there is little risk involved." This view may sound unusual, but it doesn't have to be. *If you are prepared with inner and outer resources, you stand a good chance of being able to say much the same thing to yourself some day.*

Here are some of the essential inner qualities you need:

- **Vision.** It is critical that you are able to envision your business, from start-up all the way to exit strategy. You need to know clearly what business you want to build, even if you don't know yet *how* you're going to do it! This also includes how your personal passion fits your business idea. Vision is the foundation from which everything is constructed in your business. *Ask yourself one question: Why are you going into this business?*

- **Drive.** You must be internally driven to make your vision a reality. When the going gets tough – and it will – it's dedication to your vision, along with self-motivation, that will keep you working hard to make your business profitable. It's drive – setting and achieving your goals – that propels you forward daily. *Does this sound like you?*

- **Confidence.** Unmistakable self-confidence is crucial for building your business, no matter what circumstances arise. Authentic confidence makes people respond positively, including your customers, your employees, even your competitors. *Ask yourself one question: Do you have the nerve to walk into a room full of strangers and sell them on your service?*

- **Decisiveness.** Anyone can make a decision, but as an entrepreneur you have to make smart decisions based on your best attempt to gather information. You don't have time to wait for all the facts to come in before you decide. You must develop possible solutions and begin implementing them. Then, if one doesn't work, you go on to the next. *Does this sound like you?*

- **Flexibility.** This involves a combination of originality, curiosity, and analysis. You need to be a good troubleshooter, generate many ideas, and be open to learning about and gaining expertise in areas related to your field. You must be prepared to change plans quickly, even give up your pet ideas, in order to work efficiently and produce the results you want. *Does this sound like you?*

- **Powerful Communicating.** When communicating with

customers, clients, colleagues, or vendors, ask yourself, "What do I want specifically from this conversation? How can I communicate this clearly? What does the other person want specifically?" Then listen carefully to their answer. As a business owner, you must be sensitive to others' expectations, needs, and signals, and be able to see things from their perspective – to "walk a mile in their shoes." *Does this sound like you?*

- **Results Orientation.** Getting things done is the life-blood of every business. As a SoloPreneur, you need to get things done efficiently and meet your deadlines on time. This takes careful planning, prioritizing your projects, following through, and solving problems on the spot. *Does this sound like you?*

- **Multi-Tasking.** This means wearing many hats. If there is no one to do something, you learn how or find help. It is essential to be willing to try new things, to listen to opposing ideas, and to be a quick study. If you only want to do a certain part of the business, perhaps you should think twice about starting your own. You must be willing to do many different tasks – even those you don't like! *Does this sound like you?*

- **Having an Optimistic Attitude.** High expectations equal success. Most entrepreneurs are highly motivated to succeed. They know that everything they do that is worth doing has obstacles and setbacks, just like life, and that when they experience the two-steps-forward, one-step backward syndrome, it's important to be patient enough to wait for results. It's a well-known fact that many very successful entrepreneurs had at least one failed business beforehand. Optimism also means that when you do fail, you recognize that you are not a failure, but that the strategy, product, or technique failed, and that there's most likely a better solution, which you proceed to find. *Does this sound like you?*

Happily, you don't have to excel in *all* these traits. Some traits will fit you like a glove, while others will be a stretch – but all can be developed, even if you are an accidental entrepreneur. Contrary to popular opinion, entrepreneurs are not born. If you study the lives of successful business owners, you will discover that one additional trait is their willingness to continually learn, develop themselves, and gain insight from their mistakes.

10 Traits of the Successful Entrepreneur

A SUCCESSFUL ENTREPRENEUR:

1. Is a *Risk Taker*

2. Has a *Business and Personal Vision*

3. Has *Drive and Determination*

4. Has *Self-Confidence*

5. Has *Flexibility*

6. Is a *Powerful Communicator*

7. Is a *Smart Decision-Maker*

8. Is *Action/Results Oriented*

9. Is a *Multi-Tasker*

10. Has an *Optimistic Attitude*

Do you think *you* have these traits? If so, go for it! If not, these traits can be developed. If you have a passion for doing things your way, and you have a marketable idea, you can find satisfaction and success as an entrepreneur.

CHAPTER 6:

EXERCISE: Traits of the Successful Entreprenuer

Review the **10 Traits of the Successful Entrepreneur**
on page 29. Then ask yourself,

- "Which traits do I possess?"
  Write these inside the circle (*Comfort Zone*)

- "Which traits challenge me?"
  Write these outside the circle.

Comfort Zone

List a variety of ways to develop or improve those traits that are not in your comfort zone. Talk to at least one other person to brainstorm possibilities.

How to Develop/Improve Entrepreneurial Traits

Trait 1: _____

_____

_____

Trait 2: _____

_____

_____

Trait 3: _____

_____

_____

Trait 4: _____

_____

_____

Chapter 7:

Know Why You're Going into Business

Most likely, you have taken a hard look at yourself and your finances, and you think you have what it takes to start your own business. But before you get down to the nuts and bolts of making your business a reality, ask yourself one more personal question: "What is my primary reason for starting a business?"

It is common knowledge that the first three to five years of business are critical. About half the businesses that are started fail within that time. The two factors that are mentioned most often to explain business failure are weak capitalization and poor planning. Yet when you look at successful businesses, a third reason for the failure of a business becomes clear: *the business owners have weak underlying reasons for going into business.* Having strong and meaningful reasons for going into business cement your commitment to a new enterprise and keep the business going in good and bad times.

Men's and Women's Different Motivations
Different people have widely varying reasons for going into business for themselves. Men and women, in particular, often have different motivations. Research done for the Strong Interest Inventory, a career assessment tool, suggests that men and women differ not only as to *why* they own a business, but also in the *kind* of business they choose, and in their *managerial style*, as well. So when *you* are researching your business idea or getting advice, it helps to seek out people of your own sex who already own similar businesses.

The Strong Interest Inventory measures people's interests – not their abilities or skills – by comparing their results to the results of samples of people employed in more than 100 occupations who are satisfied with their careers. One occupation that's included is a small business owner. The inventory's sample of small business owners includes such diverse businesses as professional services, consulting, retail sales, real estate, insurance, and skilled trades. The business structures include sole proprietors as well as fast-growing small companies.

In the inventory, women entrepreneurs often said that they like to work in business settings where they can organize and structure tasks or data for well-defined projects. They are results-oriented and enjoy taking charge of the practical details necessary to solve a problem quickly and efficiently. Most often, they say that they like the specific activities of running a business and want to use their best talents.

Men, on the other hand, prefer action-oriented environments, where they can work directly to produce tangible products or services and can work alone rather than supervise others. They are willing to work long hours, and most often they say that they want to earn a good income and like the specific activities of running a business.

People of both sexes tend to be enterprising types, which means they are motivated to persuade, sell, manage, and lead – all important skills when starting and running a small business. In my experience, women choose their own business more often than men do because they want to have flexible hours and make a significant contribution. They also are more likely to establish management practices, such as team management, employee autonomy, and support for work/life balance.

Common Reasons for Going into Business

Interests often influence the primary reason why a person chooses to run her or his own business. Common reasons include:

- Being your own boss.

- Earning a good income.

- Using your best skills.

- Seeing the results of your work.

- Having flexible hours.

- Experiencing the variety of day-to-day management and tasks.

- Working at home.

- Developing a business around one of your strong interests.

What's *your* reason? Be honest with yourself. If your primary reason is in reaction to a current workplace issue – for example, a personality conflict with your boss, a long commute, a low salary – it may not be enough to keep you moving through the ups and downs of starting and running a business.

Your personality, expertise, enthusiasm, and financing are all very important for success. However, *why* you want to go into business for yourself must be compelling enough to keep you committed.

Chapter 8:

Tune Up Your Entrepreneurial Skills

There are special times in life when we remember exactly where we were, what we were doing, and how we felt – sometimes, right down to the exact minute. Was this true for you when you decided to start your own business? What excited you about taking the leap? How often have you looked back on that moment and reassessed how far you've come – what went well and what needs improvement?

Reassessing your skills is like tuning up your car. When you tune up your car regularly, change the oil, and put air in the tires, the car runs pretty well. How about tuning up your entrepreneurial skills on a regular basis? Work requires three types of skills – *personal traits, transferable skills, and expertise specific to your industry or business.* Chances are that you build on your expertise daily, in the course of doing your business. Now could be a good time to reflect on your personal traits to decide what needs some improvement, so that you'll be even more successful in your business.

Personal Trait Tune-Up Assessment
Here are some entrepreneurial traits that may need
tuning up:

- **Drive.** You must be internally driven – self-motivated. A plan without commitment gets you nowhere. When the going gets tough (and it will), try to rekindle that initial spark that made you want to start a business in the first place. It's dedication to your vision and determination that will keep you working hard to make your business a success.

- **Self-Confidence.** This is the one trait that is difficult to maintain, especially when business is taking a downturn. You need unmistakable confidence in yourself and belief in your product or service. Entrepreneurs are optimistic: they know they can master challenges, bounce back from defeat, and realize goals. They may have strong egos, but they are not self-important. Even the most confident entrepreneurs ask for feedback to assess how well they are doing.

- **Adaptability.** This may well be the "mantra" of the modern workplace. You need to be a good trouble-shooter, to generate many new ideas, and to be open to learning about and gaining expertise in related areas. Be prepared to change plans quickly, even to give up your most cherished ideas, in order to work efficiently and produce the results you want. It's important to be honest, realistic, and confront mistakes, and then take steps to find workable solutions.

- **Communication.** Effective communication is essential. When communicating with your customers, clients, and colleagues, you must ask for what you want, clearly and specifically. As a business owner or consultant, you must listen first in order to be sensitive to others' expectations, needs, and signals, and figure out how to respond for maximum effect. For example, if a customer is complaining about service, you might try listening to what that person is really saying, and then work together to find a solution. If you are going to be an effective communicator, you need to empathize with others' needs and see things from their perspective – to "walk a mile in their shoes."

Taking Steps Toward Your Own Personal Tune-Up

Try the following steps for your personal tune up:

Tune In. Focus on those traits you considered in the beginning, when you first asked yourself, "Do I have what it takes to start my own business?"

- What traits did you identify? _____

  _____

- Which traits need some improvement? _____

  _____

Diagnosis. Determine your strengths and weaknesses. Pick two skills that are not up to the level you need (where you feel the current level holds you back in your business). Those are the ones that can use a tune up.

Skill #1: _____

Skill #2: _____

Create a Tune-Up Plan. Figure out what aspect of your business needs to be tweaked to improve it. Find a mentor or coach who has years of experience in business. Ask customers, colleagues, and professional contacts. Create a plan and build a support system to keep you on track.

Consider doing this tune-up every six months – for example, in January and June. Set goals. Make sure your goals are **SMART** goals: **S**pecific, **M**easurable, **A**ctionable, **R**ealistic, and within a **T**imeframe. For example: "By May 30, schedule four talks at local professional organizations." Just as your car's fuel light comes on to remind you to get gas, build in a reminder to upgrade your entrepreneurial skills on a regular basis.

PART THREE:

Taking Care of Business

CHAPTER 9:

A Name that Grows with Your Business

"What's in a name?" A great deal when it comes to the word or phrase that characterizes and brands your business. Naming your business is both exciting and difficult. The name you choose creates the image of your company. Always think about how your business will be perceived by others – customers, vendors, competitors, and the rest of the business community. You want to be taken seriously in the market-place.

How do you name your business? If you have developed your own business, the choice is yours. You want to choose a name that reflects both the essence of your business and you. If you have purchased a franchise, the decision has already been made for you. And if you have bought an existing business, you may decide to change its name. However, research this carefully so that you don't lose market share because of a name change.

> *Naming your business is both exciting and difficult. The name you choose creates the image of your company.*

No matter what type of business you're naming, consider these four points:

1. **Make sure the name fits your business.** You want customers to clearly understand what product or service you offer. For example, "JRG Associates" might indicate that the business involves consultants, but does not reveal what *type* of consulting the company offers. "Don Hayne's Automotive Shop," on the other hand, clearly says what the company does.

2. **Make sure that the company name is easy to pronounce, spell, and remember.**

3. **Make sure that the name allows for the growth of your business.** Five years into your business, you may decide to expand by adding new products and services. Make sure that your name is flexible enough to include the new additions. For example, if you start by selling candy under the name "Candy Corner," most of your products will need to be related to candy. However, if you name the business "Sweet Treats," you have many options about what to sell in your store.

4. **Research the names you are considering to make sure they are available.** Check to make sure that the name has not been previously filed in your city or county as a fictitious name, or nationally trade marked (TM), service marked (SM), or registered (®).

Before you actually make the crucial decision of a name, consider these questions:

- **Is your business local?** If your business is local and does not contain your own name as all or part of it, file a fictitious name (also known as a DBA – "Doing business as…") in your city and county. This means that no one else in your city and county should be able to use the same or similar name, usually for a period of 5 years.

- **Is your own name part of your business name?** If so, you don't need to worry about registering a fictitious name or a trademark because the name can only be yours.

- **Do you want a logo to be an integral part of your business name? Do you want to do business nationally?** If your answer is yes to one or both of these questions, you may need to consider trade marking or service marking your name and logo. A trademark (TM) is defined as "either a word, phrase, symbol, or design, or combination of words, phrases, symbols or designs, which identifies and distinguishes the source of the goods or services of one party from those of others." A service mark (SM) is the same as a trademark except that it identifies and distinguishes the source of a service.

  Remember: your fictitious name is only yours in your own city or county. Someone else can file the same name in a different county or state. The main reason to consider a trademark is to protect your name and your product/service. Also, you've probably spent a lot of time, effort, and perhaps money choosing the name and logo that is just right for you. It would be a shame for someone else to choose the same name and trademark it. It is very expensive to have to redo all of your promotional collateral and advertisements, business cards, letterhead, and signage, not to mention building up name recognition for your business again. Find out more about trademarks on the web by going to http://www.uspto.gov.

- **Do you plan to market or sell your products/services on-line?** Even if you don't plan to sell on the web, many consultants advise having a presence on the web – which means you need to have a website. It's a good idea to have as your own domain name either the actual name of your business or something close to it. Early in the naming process, make a list of prospective names and find out which of them are still available as domain names.

Remember: if your exact name is already taken as a domain name, you can add numbers or change the name in some way to make it yours. For example, "Wacky Widgets" might already be taken, but "wackywidgets123" may be available.

Be creative in naming your business – but don't rush it. Take your time. That name will be associated with you for a long time.

CHAPTER 10:

A Checklist for Setting Up Your Business

Starting your own business is exhilarating and exciting. However, there is important paperwork to contend with in order to meet and implement all the legal requirements and guidelines required to establish your business. Doing your homework in the beginning will save you costly mistakes and fewer problems after you open your business door.

For most businesses, you need to decide on your business structure, get a fictitious name (DBA, or "Doing business as…"), a business license, insurance, and pay self-employment taxes (approximately 15% of net earnings, paid quarterly) to the IRS. However, legal requirements and guidelines vary according to your type of business and location. For example, if you are manufacturing products for sale or working in the food/beverage industry, you may be required to get permits from federal, state, and local agencies. Make sure you ask an attorney as well as everyone who is in your line of business plenty of questions so you don't miss something that you need in order to "legalize" your business.

REMEMBER:
the more information you gather, the less overwhelming the paperwork will be.

[Following] is the basic information that will get you started:

Ensuring Your Business Name

If you plan to conduct business under a fictitious name, you must file a "DBA" ("Doing business as…") unless you are a corporation, in which case your name is ensured when you incorporate. In either case, you are using a name for your business that is not directly recognizable as your business because your name is not connected to it.

There are two parts to the process of filing a DBA:

1. **Filing with the County Clerk.** You must file the Fictitious Name statement with the City or County Clerk. You will receive proof from the Clerk that it has been properly recorded. Fees for this service vary between $20 and $50, and it is generally valid for four to five years.

2. **Publishing Your Fictitious Name.** Your notice of conducting business under a fictitious name must be published in a general circulation newspaper (of your choice) in the county in which your business will be located. This notice must appear in four consecutive editions. It makes sense to choose the least expensive publication in your area for this service.

Obtaining a Business License

To operate within the law, apply for a business license or permit in the city or county where your business is located. Call your city or county office to ask about local requirements. The requirements and fee structures for business licenses vary from community to community, and these licenses are taken quite seriously. The licenses provide a source of revenue for the city or county and a means of regulating the types of businesses allowed to operate within their jurisdictions. A business license is proof to the IRS that you are in business. Business licenses are renewed annually, and most cities will send you a reminder in the mail.

Seller's Permit

If you purchase items for resale or provide a taxable service, a seller's permit is required in all states where sales tax is collected. This permit means that you can collect the required sales tax on that item/service, and holds you accountable for forwarding the collected tax to the state's Department of Revenue. As the business owner, you are liable and responsible for paying the sales tax. In California, the State Board of Equalization is responsible for issuing seller's permits. For detailed information, contact your regional State Board of Equalization.

Insurance

Depending on the nature and complexity of your business, you may need a variety of insurance policies to protect you, your assets, and your customers. Think of insurance as an investment in your business. Get further information from your insurance agent. Types of insurance to consider are:

- General liability

- Professional liability (for consultants)

- Fire

- Worker's compensation (if you have employees)

- Product liability

- Health

- Key Man

- Business property

- Business interruption

Business Structures

Which type of "legal" business structure is best for you? This is an important decision – and one that you can't easily change. The three basic structures are: *sole proprietor, partnership*, and *corporation*. Each has advantages and disadvantages. There are also several types of partnerships and corporate structures to choose from. Consult an attorney or business advisor if you are in doubt.

- **Sole proprietorship.** This structure is the easiest and least expensive to establish. You are the sole owner of profits and losses. You have total control over business decisions, and you are taxed as an individual.

- **Partnership.** In this structure, two or more people agree to share ownership and management of the business. An advantage is that it gives you access to more available resources, talents, and skills. Profits and losses are shared among the partners as agreed upon. But make sure you have a written partnership agreement. Many friendships have been lost when partnerships go bad.

- **Corporation.** This is the most expensive and regulated structure. A corporation is a distinct legal entity separate from the individuals who own it. The corporation owns assets and assumes debt separate from the owners. It has the ability to raise substantial capital for growth and expansion. You are taxed twice: You pay income tax on corporate net income (profit) and on your individual salary and dividends.

Remember: the more information you gather, the less overwhelming the paperwork will be. If you proceed step by step through your checklist of requirements, this seemingly overwhelming task will be more manageable and less stressful. Build in sufficient time to complete this part of your business plan.

CHAPTER 11:

Which Business Structure is Best for You?

And now for an expanded look into business structures. The following information is offered as a general overview of your choices for the "legal structure" of your business. However, when in doubt, seek the counsel of an attorney or a business advisor.

Select your partners carefully, because you are bound by each other's decisions!

Sole Proprietorship
This is the easiest, least expensive, and most common form of business structure. A sole proprietorship is owned and operated by one person (spouses are considered as One). Sole proprietorships may have employees.

Advantages:

- *Easy* to organize.

- *You are the sole owner of the profits* (and you are also responsible for the losses).

- *Least expensive to establish.* Costs vary according to the city in which the business is formed, but usually they include a license fee and may include a business tax. Check the requirements in your city and county.

- *Less reporting.* Generally, a sole proprietorship can be established by registering your company's name (filing a DBA) and obtaining a business license.

- *No double tax…* you are taxed as an individual. Your business profit and loss is recorded on Federal Tax Form 1040, Schedule C, and the net profit or loss is transferred to your personal tax form. You will also file Schedule E, which is your contribution to Social Security. (Caution: This is equal to 15% of the net profit or loss.)

- *Total control and freedom to act.* The business is owned and operated by you.

Disadvantages:

- *Unlimited liability.* You are responsible for all business debt. This liability extends to all your assets, including your home and vehicle.

- *Less available capital.* Funding must come from the owner, and obtaining long-term financing may be difficult. Loans are based on your individual financial strength.

- *Limited growth potential.* The growth of the company is dependent upon your capabilities.

- *Death, illness, or injury can endanger the business.* The business ceases to exist as a legal entity upon the death of the owner.

Partnership

This is a legal and more formal business relationship in which two or more people agree to share ownership and management of a business.

Advantages:

- *Ease of formation.* Regulations vary by state, but generally a partnership can be established by registering the company's name (filing a DBA) and obtaining a business license.

- *Combination of resources and talents.* Two – or more – heads are better than one! A partnership allows for distribution of the workload and for sharing of ideas, skills, and responsibilities. It also makes it possible to obtain more capital and to tap into more skills.

- *Personal tax benefits.*

Disadvantages:

- *Unlimited liability.* The owners are personally responsible for the business debt. Profits must be included on each partner's individual tax return, according to their percentage of interest in the business. Further, each partner may be liable for the other's "bad business judgment." Make sure you have a written partnership agreement!

- *Lack of continuity.* The partnership terminates upon the death or withdrawal of a general partner, unless the partnership agreement provides otherwise. Death, withdrawal, or bankruptcy of one partner can endanger the entire business.

- *Relative difficulty in obtaining large sums of capital.* Long-term financing is still dependent upon review of each individual partner's assets.

- *Difficulty in disposing of the partnership interest.* The buying out of a partnership or sale to another party must be spelled out in the partnership agreement. Otherwise, the business will suffer while the dispute continues.

- *Distribution of responsibility in bankruptcy.* In case of bankruptcy, the partner with more personal assets will lose more. Be aware of this!

- *Partner's responsibility.* Select your partners carefully, because you are bound by each other's decisions! Each partner represents the company and can individually hire employees, borrow money, and operate the business.

- *Profits.* Profits are shared among the partners according to the terms outlined in your partnership agreement.

Limited Partnership

In a general partnership, the partners equally share the responsibilities associated with managing and financing the business, as well as the liability. In a limited partnership, the partners risk only their investment; and if they do not participate in the management or control of the business, they are not subject to the same liabilities as in a general partnership.

Advantages:

- *General partners have additional capital invested.*

- *Limited partners have limited liability, equal to their investment.*

- *Allocation of income and losses may provide tax benefits.*

Disadvantages:

- *Limited partners have no control over the management of the business.*

- *Partnership profits are taxed as income to the partners.*

Corporation

While the corporation is the most complex business structure of all, it can afford peace of mind for the business principals. A corporation is a distinct, legal entity, separate from the individuals who own it. It literally stands apart from the owners and is treated as an independent unit. The "corporation" owns assets and assumes debt separately from the owners.

Advantages:

- *Ownership is readily transferable.* The corporation does not cease to exist with the death of an owner, but continues operating.

- *Increased opportunities for growth and fundraising.* A corporation has access to a broader range of investors and can raise substantial capital through the sale of stock.

- *The corporation is a separate and legal entity.* It is responsible and liable for all debts. The shareholders are liable only for the amount they have invested.

- *Authority can be delegated.* The corporation has the ability to draw on the expertise and skills of more than one individual.

Disadvantages:

- *Extensive government regulations.* Corporations are complex to manage, and are highly regulated. Tedious local, state, and federal reports must be filed, and annual stockholder meetings must be held. Because of the complexity of establishing and maintaining the corporate entity, it is advisable to work with an attorney.

- *High costs to form and maintain.* The fees for setting up a corporate structure in California range from $900-$3,000. The expense for legal fees and paperwork are ongoing.

- *Increased tax load.* Income tax is paid on the corporate net income (profit) and on individual salaries and dividends. In other words, you are doubly taxed.

S Corporation

The S Corporation status allows a small business to have its income taxed to the shareholders as if the corporation were a partnership. This specifically addresses the issue of double taxation. Talk to your attorney or accountant to determine if this form of legal structure is right for your business. Specific conditions for making and maintaining an S Corporation are:

- The corporation is limited to 10 shareholders, all of which are individuals or estates.

- Only one class of stock is allowed.

- A specific portion of the corporation's receipts must be derived from active business rather than passive investments.

- No limit is placed on the size of the corporation's income and assets.

- All shareholders must consent to the election of S corporation treatment.

- The corporation must operate on a calendar year.

Limited Liability Company (LLC)

The Limited Liability Company is the newest form of business legal structure that allows owners the protection from personal liability that is provided to the corporate structure and the pass-through taxation of the partnership. Laws regarding the LLC are evolving, and some issues are complicated. Most certainly, discuss this option with an attorney and/or an accountant to determine the best course of action for your business.

CHAPTER 12:

Why a Business Plan?

Do these statements sound familiar to you?

"Why do I need a business plan?"

"Since I'm financing my own business, I don't need one because I'm not going to ask the bank for a loan."

"I know what I want to do with my business this year. I don't need to write it down."

"I know I should do it, but I don't have time to write a business plan."

Most people who are starting out or already in business think that writing a business plan is hard work. Well, they're right, it is – but it's worth it. When you do a business plan, you are creating a very specific blueprint to help you make sound business decisions and help your business prosper. After all, would you build a house without a blueprint? A business plan gives you a time line, identifies resources, outlines your goals, and details your finances and marketing plan. Having a plan can make a big difference in terms of your business success, so get your business idea out of your head and put it in writing.

A business plan gives you the following advantages:

- It helps you take an objective look at the viability of your idea.

- It clarifies your thinking and channels your energy.

- It helps you define and outline your objectives and detailed plans.

- It focuses attention on important issues and helps you set priorities.

- It keeps everyone in your company focused on your vision.

- It can be used as a feasibility study for start-up or growth.

- It can be used as a benchmark to track performance.

- It can be used as a financial proposal to present to families, banks, or investors.

Keep Your Business Plan Simple
Most often, a simple business plan will do. The only time you need an extensive business plan is if your goal is to obtain financing, in which case make sure that you fulfill all the requirements requested by the lender or investors. Otherwise, there is no need for your plan to be long and elaborate. Your vision of your business is the foundation. Imagine what your business will look like in three years. Your plan then becomes the blueprint for how to make your vision a reality and get your company where you want it to go.

To keep your plan as simple as possible, answer these basic questions:

"What are my product, program and service offerings?"

"What is my prospective target market?"

"Who are my competitors?"

"What key benefits do I offer so that customers will choose to do business with me?"

Turn the answers to these questions into your mission statement, your goals, the strategies to reach your goals, and specific projects along with dates for completion. Here are some suggestions for writing your business plan.

Write a business plan every year. The first year you are in business, your plan will reflect your best guess, based on your market research, knowledge of your industry, and product or service you offer. Your first plan will take the longest to write, but it will become a prototype for the plans that follow. The next year, writing your plan will be easier because you simply revise your original plan. You can see what worked, what didn't, and how to develop more achievable goals and accurate time lines.

Ask for help, but do not have someone else write the entire plan for you. If you do, you won't develop the direct, hands-on relationship with your business that you need. However, you do not need to write the plan alone. Involve members of your staff. Ask for feedback from colleagues. Hire a consultant to keep you on track.

Don't spend more time than you need on your business plan. It doesn't need to take days to write.

Print copies of your business plan for everyone in your organization. Make sure that everyone reads it, understands it, and gets behind it. Treat it like a living document. If the time line proves to be unreasonable three months into the year, revise it and adjust the completion dates. One purpose of the plan is to help you track how well you are doing what you said you were going to do. There are consultants, resources and books that you can use to help you write a business plan. One of the most helpful books is *The One Page Business Plan* by Jim Horan. It is written in a workbook format and simplifies the process.

Chapter 13:

Exercise: Target Your Market!

Once you have done your exploratory market research, you are ready to zero in on your particular target market. The following exercise will help you clarify the best segment(s) within your target market for your product or service.

Target Market Worksheet

1. Questions to Help Determine Your Customer Target Market(s)

"Who are my customers? What do I know about them?" (i.e., economic level, lifestyle, sex and age range, income level, buying habits)

_____

_____

"Where are my customers located? Where do they live, work, currently shop? What problems do they want solved?"

_____

_____

"What is the projected size of the market? What percentage of the total market could be mine?"

_____

_____

"What do my customers both need and want?"

_____

_____

"How can I meet those needs? What are the specific ways in which my business will benefit my customers?"

_____

_____

"What is unique about my business? Why will these customers buy from *me*?"

_____

_____

Key Issue for innovative entrepreneurs:
*"What does my product/service/idea
offer to a marketplace that has
somehow managed without it so far?"*

---

2. Key Questions to Ask, Based on Your Research:

"Is there sufficient market potential for my business to be successful?"

_____

_____

"Do I and/or my company possess the expertise and resources needed to create the required products and services? If not, what would I need and how would I obtain it?"

_____

_____

"Is there enough profit potential?"

_____

_____

Chapter 14:

Your Business from A to Z

You've just launched your new business. You have a great business plan. You've researched your market. You have a great location for your business. You've developed your pricing strategies – *and* you have a killer marketing plan. What else do you need to succeed?

Here are some helpful, practical tips from A to Z to help you grow a profitable, sustainable business.

A - **Adapt quickly to changes.** This is the "mantra" of the modern workplace. Be prepared to change plans quickly, even give up your pet ideas, in order to work efficiently and produce the results you want.

B - **Believe in yourself.** You are the idea and business generator. *You* make your business happen.

C - **Customer service.** Today, quality customer service makes you stand out. It's easy to duplicate a product or type of service, but not so easy to duplicate loyal customers.

D - **Decide whether or not you will need to hire extra help** to complete the project on time. Don't forget to add the extra cost to your proposal at the beginning of a project.

E - **Establish connection with professional or trade associations in your field** for contacts, referrals, and support.

F - Financing. Unless your business is a candidate for venture capital, it will be financed by you, your family and friends, and possibly your bank. Have enough money on hand to support a minimum of 6 to 12 months of living expenses to start. It's hard to grow a business when you're worried about paying the mortgage. For example, if your business is a professional service, it can take 3 to 5 years to make a substantial profit.

G - Give back to the community in which you do business. For example, volunteer on a local non-profit board, donate goods and services to a school auction, or coach a soccer team.

H - Hire an accountant as soon as you can afford it. Know where the money is *really* going.

I - Invest in technology that helps your office run efficiently. Today, a home office can be as technologically sophisticated as one in a large corporation.

J - Jargon: Avoid it. Sell the benefits of your product or service without using overly technical language.

K - Keep it simple. Make the benefits and process of doing business with you easy for your customers.

L - Lighten up. You've done serious work to launch your business. Make sure you find time for family, friends, and fun.

M - Maximize your advertising dollars. Pick the ad venues that bring in the most business, and stick with those.

N - Niche your business. Create and communicate what's unique and special about doing business with you.

O - Organize yourself daily with "To Do" lists, a contact management system, and whatever else keeps you working efficiently so that you can increase your billable hours.

P - **Play at work.** It's no mystery why start-up companies offer recreational facilities.

Q - **Question constantly.** "What works?" "What needs improvement?" "How can I position this product better?"

R - **Remember the 80-20 rule**: 80% of your business comes from 20% of your customers. Make sure you reach those 20% frequently.

S - **Support is essential**, especially from your family. You can't do it all alone.

T - **Talk to your competitors.** They're the best source of market information and trends.

U - **Use all available resources** to stay ahead of the market curve.

V - **Voicemail.** Make sure you have a professional, friendly message. Change it frequently as your schedule changes to let your customers know when they can expect to reach you. Return calls promptly.

W - **"We," as in "We would be happy to provide that service for you!"** Even if you are a sole proprietor, using the proverbial "we" makes your company sound bigger.

X - **X-pect success.** A positive, optimistic attitude is infectious. Your colleagues and customers will notice.

Y - **Your web site** gives you a national and international presence for business opportunities. It also can serve as your online brochure, which is quick, easy, and inexpensive to update.

Z - **Zzzzz** peacefully at night. You've done a great job.

CHAPTER 15:

Put Your Own Money on the Line: Investing and Financing

Whenever my son asks me to buy something expensive for him, I always ask him one question before I decide whether to buy it: "If you had enough of your own, would you be willing to spend your own money on this?" The key words here are "willing" and "your own money." If he says yes, I will consider his request seriously. Why? Because this is something he really wants, not something he thinks might be cool to own. Because he wants it enough to put his money where his mouth is.

This is a key question to ask yourself when you are considering starting your own business. If your business is funded with your own hard-earned money rather than other people's money, your chance of succeeding goes way up. "More than 80% of new entrepreneurs start their businesses without any commercial loans or debt financing. In order to not saddle themselves with debt, they often choose to obtain their initial financing from their own savings, from friends and family members, informal investors, or home equity loans."(Small Business Administration, www.sba.gov)

Funding a business with your own money means that you will not go into business on a whim or just try it to see how it goes. It means that you have limited financial resources of money, and you know what it took to earn it. Your first business expense probably won't be a fancy new car. Perhaps it will be a new computer and an accounting system instead. After all, you have limited money, time, and energy to invest in your business, and you need all three to succeed – each week, month, and year.

Questions to Consider

Whatever source of financing you use, here are questions to consider when you are doing your financial planning for your new business:

- What will your start-up costs be?

- Will there be slow seasons each year? How will customers pay you – every 30 days, 60 days, 90 days, or on some other basis?

- What kind of variable expenses do you project (e.g., direct labor, materials, commission, advertising)?

- What will your fixed expenses be (e.g., rent, utilities, leased equipment, payroll)?

- What salary or owner's draw do you need each month to support yourself? Your salary or draw should be enough to cover your monthly budgeted fixed expenses, such as your mortgage, rent, car payments, food, etc. Rule of thumb: It's best to have 6 months to 1 year of living expenses available for your first year of business.

- What is your best estimate of your sales and expenses, month by month, for the first year of your business? What is your break-even projection? Your profit projection?

- Once you have run the numbers for your new business based on questions like those above, ask yourself, "How long will it take to achieve my break-even point?" Then ask, "How long will it take me to make my projected profit once I reach my break-even point?" Be conservative.

- In the first year of business, how realistic is it for you to attract the number of customers you need to break even and make a profit?

- How many clients do you need to see a month?

- How many widgets do you need to sell a month? You will be surprised how many items you need to sell just to break even. In order to make a profit, you need to sell a whole lot more than that. For example, if you are a consultant working from your home office and you've figured that your overhead is $2,000/month and you want an income of $60,000 annually or $5000/month the first year, this means that you need to have $7,000 worth of billable hours/month. If you charge $100 per hour, you need to have 70 client hours a month or, 3.5 client hours per day.

New entrepreneurs say, "Yes! I would love to work only 3.5 hours per day!" However, what will it actually take to generate this number of client hours? Depending on your business, it might take 2 hours of marketing for 1 hour of billable work, especially when you're in the start-up phase. Add in slow times of the year (such as the Christmas holidays), administrative time, and the fact that you are probably doing all the business tasks yourself during the first year, and you will discover that you probably won't have much time to lounge by the pool.

However, there might be a time when you need to finance your business, either through a bank loan or investors – in other words, a time when you need a large sum of money that you can't pull out of your business or savings. Common reasons for financing include inventory, equipment and fixed assets, and working capital shortages. If you want to retain total control in running your business, obtain debt financing – a loan from a bank, family or friends. Another option is equity financing, in which you give investors a percentage of your business profits and/or a say in how to manage your business in return for their money.

Careful planning and realistic financial projections can make or break your business. To be truly successful, you need to pay close attention to the details in order to sustain your business and reach the profits you envision.

PART FOUR:

What Do *You* Bring to the Party?

Chapter 16:

Beyond Making Money, What Motivates You?

As I watched the fireworks last July 4th, it struck me that Independence Day – which marks the birth of our country in 1776, then a struggling, intrepid, individualistic new nation – embodies the entrepreneurial spirit. The Declaration of Independence, symbolizing the motivation to build a country that promotes "life, liberty and the pursuit of happiness," reminds me of the mission statement that new entrepreneurs struggle to write when they are giving "birth" to a business venture – a daunting task filled with challenges and risks, yet exciting and full of hope. Just as our entrepreneurial forefathers were determined to build a new life for themselves in America, today's entrepreneurs are highly motivated to succeed.

Clearly, making money is a large motivation. Aside from making money, though, what motivates you to go into your own business?

Once I gave a talk at a conference on the four most common motivators for entrepreneurs: Creativity, Control, Challenge, and Cash. The audience responded by spontaneously suggesting other words beginning with the letter "C" that motivated them in their work. Since then, I have been thinking about and experiencing these motivators in my own business and my work with clients. Here is my list of motivational "C" words and how each impacts the entrepreneurial lifestyle. I invite you to define each word in the way that's most meaningful to you.

Challenge. If this is your motivator, you love the exhilaration of succeeding at a particularly hard task, inventing a new product, or finding a fun way to market your service.

You like to work on projects that provide opportunities to try new approaches. You love learning and are willing to take calculated risks frequently.

Control. If this is your primary motivator, you want to be the lead dog. You're a take-charge kind of person. You are interested in every aspect of your business. Often, the lines between business and play are blurred because you are your business.

Creativity. If this is your motivator, you are innovative and independent, with high energy and strong self-confidence. You also like to tackle situations or problems and find creative ways to solve them. You thrive on tackling projects that might involve unknown difficulties or have outcomes that are unpredictable.

Cash. You love making lots of money and may also be motivated by achieving status and prestige. If this is your number-one motivator, choose a business that has a strong likelihood of growing fast. Otherwise, if you aren't making a healthy profit within the first two years, you'll lose interest.

Contribution. If this is your primary motivator, you want to make a difference or help others improve their lives in both personal and practical ways. This could be anything from founding a non-profit, to direct aid to third-world countries, to being an auto mechanic who goes out of your way to make an emergency repair on a customer's car.

Competition. If this is your primary motivator, you want to be the best at what you do. Being competitive in the marketplace is essential to keeping your business doors open, but for you it is also a strong internal motivator. You strive to be the market leader in your field.

Collaboration. If this is your primary motivator, you enjoy developing a special synergy with a group of colleagues to create a strategic alliance or a new product or service. You want to brainstorm with trusted colleagues for inspiration, validation of your efforts, encouragement, and renewed energy. If you have employees, you will promote teamwork and a free exchange of ideas.

Business owners usually have two to three internal drivers that motivate them to start and run their own business. Of course, you need to be competitive and make a profit in order to have a viable business; but, usually there is one additional motivator that drives you. When I'm trying to find out what makes people tick I often ask, "What really excites you about what you do?" Answer that question for yourself, and you'll know what your strongest motivators are. Apply those to your business, and you have a great chance of succeeding at something you love doing.

Chapter 17:

Exercise: What are Your Key Motivators?

Entrepreneurs are people who are highly motivated to succeed. Here are some of the most common motivators that impact the entrepreneurial lifestyle.

Try This Exercise

All motivation is internally driven. Each person usually has 2 to 3 strong motivators. What are yours? Choose your strong motivators from the list below and write your own definitions for each. (If your strong motivators do not appear on this list, add them in the spaces below.)

☑ CASH_____

_____

☑ CREATIVITY _____

_____

☑ CHALLENGE _____

_____

☑ COLLABORATION _____

_____

☑ CONTROL _____

_____

☑ COMPETITION _____

_____

☑ CONTRIBUTION _____

_____

☑ _____

_____

☑ _____

_____

☑ _____

_____

_____

Describe how your key motivators might complement each other to create optimal satisfaction and productivity in your business.

☑ _____

_____

_____

_____

_____

_____

_____

CHAPTER 18:

If You're the Boss,
Who Keeps *You* Accountable?

When you work for someone else, you may not always appreciate having a boss. Yet one good thing about a boss is that this person keeps you on track and accountable. But who keeps you accountable when *you* are *your own* boss?

Let's look at what it means to be accountable. The dictionary defines accountability as "considered to be responsible and answerable." In other words: You're in charge. You get to take the credit (and the blame) for what happens in your business.

It's no wonder that the most frequent reason given for starting a business is "being my own boss" – fulfilling the dream of pursuing your own ideas and being *in control* rather than *under someone else's control*. Once you're in business for yourself, however, you realize that along with the control comes accountability. When the going gets tough – and it will – will you opt for the beach? Or will you be accountable by pushing on with the business of your business? This means dealing with all the nuts and bolts of growing a business: writing and reviewing your business or marketing plan, learning your product better, minding your accounting, keeping up with market trends, adding skills, staying visible in your field, and achieving your goals. Here's a simple system you may want to adopt to achieve your goals so that you can be accountable to your business and still go to the beach – but without a guilty conscience.

Think it:

Decide what you need to accomplish, and set priorities for your objectives.

Write it:

In a journal, write your goals and put your action steps, or tasks, into the categories listed on the following page. This gets your plans out of your head, on paper, and into action.

Speak it:

Tell at least three people you see regularly what you plan to do. At some point, you will see one of those people, and they'll ask: "How's your new product going?" This makes your plan real and motivates you to follow through.

Complete it:

Set completion dates for each task in each category. If you know what your tasks are and when you want to have them done, you are much more likely to do them. I can't tell you how powerful this is. Thinking is the beginning of possibility. Every great accomplishment starts with an idea or thought. When you write your own thoughts, ideas and plans, they become more real and actionable. If you add telling people about your plans, you increase your accountability. This motivates you to meet your goals.

The following categories provide one way to set priorities for necessary tasks:

Have to do it now.
These are things you must do right away, or you'll suffer serious consequences, like losing that big account.

Important, but can do it later.
For example, a thank-you note to a colleague who referred business to you, updating your web site, or preparing for a sales presentation.

Have to do it regularly.
These are the maintenance and clerical tasks that need to be done. However, don't let yourself get bogged down with them. Schedule a certain amount of time during the week to do these tasks, and stick to it.

Time wasters.
Those tasks that others want you to do, but are not your top priority. That stuff on your desk that you think you might use someday, but haven't looked at for months. These are the tasks you can take off your "to-do" list.

At different times, the same task can fit into any of these categories. For example, I have one talk that I give frequently. Each time I give it, I change it slightly to fit the audience. Consequently, I have several renditions of the agenda, overheads, and handouts.

The first time I made this presentation, this task fell into the top category, "Have to do it now." After I'd given the talk 10 times, the presentation materials fell into the "important, but can do it later" category. However, when I was about to give this presentation recently, it fell into the "have to do it now" category again because I needed to totally reorganize the materials into a new notebook.

Now the presentation materials fall into the "do it regularly" category, because I can update them very easily and quickly. Before I reorganized the materials, however, they fell into the "time wasters" category because I had to sort through a pile of materials each time I gave the presentation.

Chapter 19:

Making Procrastination Work for You

Procrastination is the opposite of time management. Solo business owners must juggle shifting priorities daily. They are the ultimate practitioners of multi-tasking. How do they do it? The answer is they don't, always. They procrastinate. Being your own boss is great – until you realize that you are the only one who truly knows what your weekly "To Do" list contains. It's easy to tell yourself that you'll do it tomorrow.

I suggest that you put into your weekly plan both the practice of time management and of conscious procrastination, and establish an accountability system that will help you check off items on your "To Do" list –

Think of procrastination as a way to build balance into your life.

and still have some fun. Think of procrastination as a way to build balance into your life. A tongue-in-cheek definition of an entrepreneur is someone who would rather work 80 hours a week for himself than 40 hours a week for someone else. But sometimes those 60-80 hours turn into 90 hours, with at least 5-10 of them wasted on procrastination. Instead of worrying about procrastinating, put open space in your calendar to create time to do things you like that are unrelated to work. Worry makes you anxious and unproductive. Open time allows you to do things you like and can be a time for creativity or relaxation, to help you feel rejuvenated.

One of my clients recently decided to read a novel for 30 minutes each day. In the first week, she managed to read the novel for 2 hours on Sunday and 15 minutes on Tuesday, Thursday, and Friday. She acknowledged that she didn't reach her goal, but she had gotten started. By the second week, she read 30 minutes each day except on Saturday and Sunday. By the third week, she was so hooked by the novel that she read one hour every day and finished the book. I asked her whether reading the book helped or hindered her work schedule. To her surprise, she said that she got more done for her business on the third week. Upon reflection, she realized that she was more focused and efficient the third week because she wanted to continue reading the book and didn't waste time thinking about getting her work done; she just did it. There is an old saying: If you want something done, ask a busy person to do it.

Procrastination has a negative connotation, but here's how you can make it work for you:

On Sunday evening or Monday morning, write your "To Do" list for the week. Decide how much time you normally procrastinate. Allow 2 hours for pure procrastination, according to your regular modus operandi. Then decide what you would like to do that week that is not related directly to your business. Prioritize your workload for the week; estimate the hours needed to get it all done; then, determine how many hours you have left for "fun."

Next, divide that time into "family time," "social engagements," and your "private time." Don't worry about family time and social engagements; they will find their way into your calendar. Work with the amount of time you have left for "private time." Then schedule "private time" into your daily calendar as you see fit. You may find that some days you have 30 minutes before bedtime or 20 minutes on BART. Why not plan those times as carefully as you do your business meetings? The other way to do it is to leave the time open, so that you can do just what you feel like doing at that time.

For those of you who don't like so much structure, be ready to take advantage of unexpected free time. For example, last week I was preparing for a class I planned to teach the next week when I got a phone call saying that the organization had decided not to offer the class for two more weeks. That phone call freed up my calendar for one evening that week and one the next week. So instead of preparing for the class, I went out to dinner with friends, whom I hadn't been able to get together with for a while.

However you choose to deal with procrastination, if you don't manage your time well, you may never actually enjoy those things you love to do (besides growing your business).

Chapter 20:

What Stops You in Your Tracks: Self-Sabotage and Resistance

Let's face it: sometimes, although it's the last thing on your conscious mind, you sabotage your own plans. For example, you have a plan, but you aren't taking the action steps you need to follow through and reach your goal.

Why would people sabotage their own good intentions? Resistance, fear, and that voice inside that never has anything good to say to you about yourself! Perhaps you don't want to admit that you don't know how to do something; or, perhaps you're not letting yourself do what it takes to sell yourself and your services.

Resistance

There are reasons why you resist what you really want. There are payoffs. It's much easier to keep doing what you already know how to do, what you're comfortable doing. People often choose safety and security over making changes because they don't want to face their feelings of fear and limitation. At least the current circumstances are familiar. It is a human habit to continue doing what you are used to doing, even if you don't like it, because it's the pattern you know. When you don't take a risk, you can couch your resistance in the guise of being "responsible," "practical," and "reliable."

TRY THIS EXERCISE to move you past your resistance.

1. **Ask yourself:** "How much do I want to stick with my belief that 'I can't do _____'"? Fill in the blank with your most common "I can't."

_____

2. **Activity:** What is the particular change you are contemplating? E.g., a new business opportunity, a new sales promotion, a speaking engagement, etc. Write it in the blank:

_____

3. **Loss vs. Gain:**
   Make a list of everything you think you will lose or gain from this change.

   Loss   _Gain_

   _____   _____

   _____   _____

   _____   _____

   _____   _____

   _____   _____

   _____   _____

   _____   _____

   _____   _____

   _____   _____

Which list is longer? If your Loss list is much longer than your Gain list, perhaps it's just as well *not* to make this change. If your Gain list is at least as long as or longer than your Loss list, get off the couch and get going!

However, it's essential to re-evaluate your lists. For each item on your Loss list, ask yourself, "Am I willing to give this up?" And for each item on your Gain list, ask yourself, "How important is this item to me and my business?" Then ask, "Are there any more items to add to my Gain list? Perhaps there is something you didn't put on the Gain list, because you felt it was too silly, too scary, or too huge? Put it on the list!

Then, after this evaluation, if the payoff is worth the effort, keep going. When it's not, stop!

Make Friends with Your Inner Critic

Your Inner Critic is another big obstacle. Your Critic sabotages you constantly. He/she says things like:

"I need to stick with what I know best. I can't do this!"

*"I'm not a good public speaker,
and speaking is essential for this project."*

"I don't have much to offer because I'm new in my field."

Sound familiar? You'll notice that the Critic comments on everything you do and everything you haven't done yet. One thing you can count on: the messages are always bad. The Inner Critic is bad news, because your brain believes what you tell it about yourself. It's very easy to believe those negative messages from your Critic, and you will act as if those messages are true.

The good news is that you can reprogram the Critic in your head to give you positive and supportive messages instead of negative and defeating ones.

Here's how:

- Tune into your Critic and listen to what its voice says.

- Write down some of the things your Critic says to you. Ask yourself: "Is that true?"

- Turn each criticism into an encouraging statement (often called an *affirmation*).

- Write 2 or 3 affirmations on index cards. Say and write them on a daily basis. Some experts say to do this 10-12 times a day. You won't believe them at first. It takes practice and time to quiet your Inner Critic. But don't worry. You will begin to believe your positive self-talk.

- Practice your positive statements every day for a month. You'll be happily surprised at the results!

The number-one reason people buy from you is that you are CONFIDENT! If *you* believe in you, so will your customers!

Chapter 21:

The Isolation of the "SoloPreneur"

Isolation is one of the unforeseen difficulties encountered by the new entrepreneur, especially consultants or home-based business folks. Once their business is running, entrepreneurs find themselves spending more time alone than expected. This is especially true for people who most recently worked in a large corporation. Those informal meetings, talks with colleagues, and team projects are not possible in their current setting.

They also discover they are spending time on administrative tasks that others used to handle. Often, this additional workload cuts into the time that otherwise would be available to spend with family and friends. Growing the business comes first, and social activities get put on the back burner. This is understandable – but it also adds to feeling isolated.

Making Supportive Connections
If this is true for you, the good news is: there is no need to be a lone wolf. Take action by making connections and building a support network. You will find that this network will nurture you and your business in many unforeseen ways – not just with business referrals, but with new ideas, accountability, solutions to problems, and a safe group to talk about what's really going on in your business. One way to connect is to start your own business support group. There are many networking events and professional organizations in major cities that you can attend. These are good sources for developing contacts and creating an informal support group of your own. Invite one like-minded person to help you start a business support network.

The goal is for members to feel comfortable discussing all aspects of their business, setting goals, and providing accountability for each other. Request that your colleague recruit one other business owner to join your group, and you do the same. Once you have at least four members, schedule your initial meeting at a convenient, neutral location. A local restaurant or coffeehouse works well. (This eliminates one person always feeling responsible for providing the office and refreshments.) At the first meeting, form a consensus on the ground rules for your group and ask for a commitment of at least four months. Be specific about the needs and motivations of each member, so that everyone can see how this group will benefit them. A small group of four to six works best. Time and money are precious to new business owners. For a group to be successful, members need to see how spending time away from earning money benefits their business. It can't be just a nice social visit to avoid feeling lonely.

Your support network will develop its own character over time, keep you connected, and provide surprising benefits.

My most successful business support group was formed to help each member market her business. We have been meeting once a month for six years. There are four women, all in private practice – career consulting, business coaching, body-work, and psychotherapy. We still discuss marketing ideas, but it has evolved into much more. We cheer each other through our successes and support each other through our failures; we test out new ideas before we unveil them publicly; we set goals and keep each other accountable; we laugh, as well as share practical tips and contacts; and as a result, we have developed a mutual trust.

Your support network will develop its own character over time, keep you connected, and provide surprising benefits. If forming or participating in a network is not for you, try renting an office in a shared-services office building. There are many opportunities to schmooze with other business owners in the building, much like chatting with folks from other units in a large company.

You can also try talking weekly with a good friend. Tell each other your goals for the next week. Agree to check up on each other to see if you have achieved your goals. Build regular exercise into your work week – at the health club, on the tennis court, walking with a friend, or jogging on the beach. It gives you a change of pace, fresh air, and energy.

No matter how busy you are, spend time with your family and friends every week. Attend social activities that you enjoy!

Join your local Chamber of Commerce and serve on a committee, building contacts in your community. Go beyond "Let's exchange business cards." Get to know people, develop relationships, and offer assistance – and opportunities will naturally evolve. People want to refer business to people they know and trust.

CHAPTER 22:

Burnout: How to De-Stress

Do you lie awake at night feeling anxious, but you don't know why? Do you wake up in the morning and dread going to work? Is the excitement of being your own boss gone?

Does this sound familiar? Doing something you love and being your own boss are probably the biggest reasons you chose self-employment. Yet the other side of the coin may be the stress you feel about meeting your own high expectations for business success.

Jeff, the owner of a successful small manufacturing company, was lying awake one night thinking about work, when he noticed that his body felt tense and rigid, and that his heart was beating rapidly.

Sometimes, a simple change in attitude makes all the difference.

He was alarmed. "Why am I feeling so anxious?" Jeff asked himself. "I've just completed my best year in business, and my personal life is great. Yet why am I feeling physically ill?" The next day he saw his doctor, who confirmed that Jeff had high blood pressure. The doctor put him on medication with the suggestion that he take some time off and try to relax. As Jeff was leaving, he thought, "How can I do that?" Gradually, he realized that all along, he felt guilty about taking time off for himself. Consequently, he'd taken only two real vacations in ten years. After much soul searching and careful analysis of his business practices, Jeff decided to change how he managed his company – and himself.

Jeff instituted two significant changes at his company. First, he delegated more of the day-to-day responsibilities of running the business to one of his six employees. This put one layer of management between himself and production.

Second, Jeff decided to be less of a manager and more of a leader. He developed long-range goals and gradually took charge of scheduling production, so that he was able to spend more time planning than playing catch-up. For himself, he discovered simple ways he could take time off without feeling guilty. Currently, some of his favorite activities to unwind are: taking longer lunches on beautiful days; playing computer games 10 to 15 minutes each day; and learning to play the guitar.

If this scenario sounds familiar, consider some of the following ways to reduce stress.

Reshape Your Attitude

Recently, I saw a bumper sticker that said, "Attitude is everything." I agree: attitude is the most essential component of making positive change. Your attitude is always noticed by others and reacted to accordingly. You may not have control over time, orders, customer demands, or your teenage son, but you do have control over your own attitude. A positive one is simply more productive and more fun. Sometimes, a simple change in attitude makes all the difference.

Delegate Work to Others

One of the common mistakes of owners who are growing their businesses is keeping too much control. After all, they got where they are by doing it all. But often, they don't know when to stop working: 60-80 hours per week are commonplace. However, there is a time in all businesses when doing too much yourself is detrimental to you and your business. Know when to delegate tasks, decisions, and responsibility to others on your staff, or when to hire outside help. Keep an overview of operations, and remove yourself from handling some of the day-to-day details. This frees you to spend more time doing what you intend to do best – building a profitable business.

Stress-Reducing Activities

- Take up a hobby – tap-dancing, gardening, volleyball. Many business owners say there aren't enough hours in the day to do their business tasks, let alone spend time on a hobby. However, a hobby can provide new focus, fun, and relaxation. Doing something you enjoy is one of the best stress-reducers.

- Take mini-breaks during the work day. Take a nap, read a book, walk around the block, or sit silently for 10 minutes, doing nothing. Schedule time each day to do something for yourself that is unrelated to business.

- Schedule a vacation. Pick a traditionally slow time of year in your business. Plan a vacation to a place that you find relaxing. Buy non-refundable airline tickets so you won't be tempted to cancel at the last minute. Many business "emergencies" can be handled by someone other than you. Also, resist the temptation to take your cell phone and fax machine on vacation with you. Leave your business at home.

Look carefully at yourself and your business, and take heed from Jeff's experience. Find ways to put excitement, healthy challenge, and fun back into your business life. Learn to recognize when your stress level is too high. Take two of the above suggestions, and listen to your business coach.

Chapter 23:

How Do You Spell Success?

What makes a business successful? Who decides that it is successful? How do you define success? What measures do you use to determine success? It is a good idea to look into this subject before deciding where you fit on the scale. Success includes intrinsic satisfaction, as well as financial rewards.

Looking Back
Whether you're just starting out in business or have been in business for years, it's a good idea to take stock and acknowledge yourself at least once a year in terms of what you think makes you and your business successful.

TRY THIS EXERCISE: Look back over the year so far. What goals have you met that make you feel successful? Write down three, then examine each and write about what you did to accomplish each. Ask yourself questions such as:

- "What new ideas did I implement, and which ones haven't I implemented yet?"

- "What's stopping me?"

- "What worked really well this year?"

- "What values drive my business?"

- "How can I expand upon my strengths and successes?"

- "What are the objectives and benchmarks I put in place to accomplish my goals?"

- "What made me laugh?"

- "Why am I in this business?"

- "What project was the most exciting and fun?"

Looking Forward

However, sometimes it's easier to define success not by looking back, but by looking ahead at what you want to accomplish and determining possible success factors.

TRY THIS EXERCISE: Imagine that it is December 31st, and you have thrown a party to celebrate your business' success. Brainstorm three accomplishments you would like to be celebrating. Imagine walking up to the microphone to acknowledge your business successes. You might say: "I'm proud to announce the publishing of my book." Or, "We successfully completed the roll-out of our new product line in August! Sales have already surpassed our projections." Or, "I doubled my conference keynote speaking engagements this year." Which of your dream accomplishments do you want to aim for?

Imagination is the beginning of possibility. Every great accomplishment starts with an idea or a thought. Sometimes the wildest ideas can lead to a breakthrough in your business.

Next Steps:

- Look at all areas of your business. Which areas do you want to focus on to achieve your goals? Marketing and sales? Operations? Financials? R&D? Human Resources? Choose one or two areas, and write objectives for achieving your goal(s) in that area. A good objective needs to be specific, measurable, realistic, and set in time. For example, an objective for a catalogue business might be: "Ship 98% of orders the same day and 100% of orders within 3 days, consistently, by November 30th." This objective can be graphed and will show you, on a weekly basis, how close to your goal you are. If you see that you are falling behind, you can troubleshoot, make appropriate changes, and move forward.

- Create objectives for achieving your goals that can be measured, and then check your results monthly throughout the year.

- Don't forget to consider personal goals as well. As a business owner, it is very easy to work long hours and let go of leisure activities, hobbies, or community service. Look at what you like to do besides business, and make room and time for these activities in your schedule. For example, commit to working 50 hours per week and playing on three out of four weekends; or, commit to reading one fiction book a month; or mentor a young person in your community who is interested in learning about business.

The dictionary defines success as: "The favorable or prosperous termination of attempts or endeavors." How do *you* spell success? Here is one way:

S = **S**ell by building relationships and offering solutions to customers' needs.

U = **U**nderstand your market and find your unique niche.

C = **C**reate value.

C = **C**ontrol the sails of your business ship, not the wind.

E = **E**xpect success.

S = **S**upport your efforts by asking for help when you need it and giving it when asked.

S = **S**tart small and think big.

Chapter 24:

A Fork in the Road: Which Way Do You Go?

It's April. Your taxes are done. You have a clear picture of how well your business did in the previous year.

So, what's next? Are you planning to continue going in the same direction? Or do you want to add or change a new service or product? This could be a good time to tweak your business plan for the third quarter of the year. In order to grow your business, it's important to invest your time, money, and energy where it will do the most good.

Adding a new service or product, hiring a new employee, or changing your marketing mix can seem overwhelming at first. Change requires making some hard decisions. When you reach your initial growth goals for your business, it's time to move to the next level. This can be daunting for the solo operator: "What if I make the wrong decision?" "How do I research the market?" "How confident am I about making this change?" "Do I have the time and energy to learn quickly what I need to know to make my new venture successful?"

But there are ways not to get overwhelmed. Remember, don't be a lone wolf. Get some help. Talk to someone about the fears you have regarding expanding your business. Somehow, when you share your fears with others, they become lighter and more manageable.

For example, one of my clients is a real estate investor. He wants to diversify his real estate holdings, but he is not sure how to do it. If he sells one of his apartment buildings, he will incur heavy taxes unless he reinvests the proceeds into a similar type of investment, but his dilemma is that he doesn't want to buy another apartment building. What type of commercial property might he consider that will require less intensive on-site management responsibilities and will afford a reasonable rate of return on his investment? I suggested that he might find this problem less daunting and easier to deal with if he looked at it like a project. Then, I gave him a simple plan and asked him to check back with me in a few weeks.

At the end of two weeks, he called to tell me that he had decided to purchase a 45-unit building in another state with a solid expanding rental market. I was surprised, because he had been so sure that he didn't want another apartment building. However, his research convinced him that it would work out, because he could hire a property-management company to deal with the day-to-day, on-site management. He discovered that he needed to diversify in terms of location, rather than type of property. He is now ready to sell one building and buy another larger one in a different state.

Treat the Change Like a Project

If you are at a crossroads in your business, it will be easier if you treat the change like a project. Follow these simple rules to make the change happen.

1. **Know what you want to do.** Carefully research the change you are considering. What will it take to make the change? Will you need to hire a new employee? Can you partner with a colleague? Is there really a market for what you want to do? Make a decision based on your research.

2. **Plan what you're going to do.** Develop a plan to implement your new service, product, or process. Set benchmarks to check your progress, including a cut-off date for canceling the project if it proves not to be feasible.

3. **Do what you have to do.** Follow through on your plans. Make adjustments as needed. Get input from other people in your field, or a business consultant, if appropriate. Fold this project into your other responsibilities. Don't

lose sight of the services/products you are already offering. Be realistic about the length of time it will take to complete this new project.

4. **Document what you did.** Keep written notes of your progress. Note what worked well and what didn't. Determine the pitfalls of your new venture. Keep a "good ideas" files to capture ideas that come up and that you might want to try later. Use your documentation to evaluate the viability of taking the necessary next steps in your plan.

5. **Evaluate and make appropriate changes.** Now that you've done your research, tested the market, and followed your plan, it's time to decide if you are going to implement your new idea or not. You have solid information on which to base an intelligent decision. If you decide to go for it, make any necessary changes and move forward. If you decide not to do it, you have learned a great deal and discovered new ideas that you may want to try at a later date. Next time you are at a crossroads, you'll have a better idea of what to do to grow your business successfully.

CHAPTER 25:

Tips from Seasoned Entrepreneurs

"What do you want to be when you grow up?" As a child, you may have answered: "a lawyer," "a teacher," "a doctor," "a race car driver." As an adult, you may have asked yourself the same question and answered, "I want to start my own business." In either case, it might help you to follow the advice I got from my Dad as a teenager: "Whatever you decide to be, be the best one you can be." There is a direct correlation between being really good at what you do and being happy in your work.

Good Advice Isn't Cheap
When you start a business, most people advise you to develop a specialty or a particular niche in your area of the marketplace. This is a definite advantage; however, as a small business owner, especially a one-person business, you must learn to wear many hats just to keep your business going on a daily basis. When I was starting my private practice, one seasoned entrepreneur I know advised me to be "an amazing juggler." There are so many projects you will have going at once that it's like a balancing act.

It goes without saying that you'll invest time, money, and effort into your business. But don't forget to invest in yourself – outside of business. Cultivate your other interests. Adding to your expertise in your field makes perfect sense; however, you may think you're just too busy running a business to garden, bike, travel, or join a social club. Why pursue these interests? Because you enjoy them! Doing things you like also makes sound business sense. If you have a wide range of interests and activities, you are more interesting to others, and you can talk about a variety of topics with people you meet. In addition, you often get the best ideas in the most unlikely places – for example, you may get a solution to a nagging business problem just as you're teeing off at the 9th hole.

It isn't surprising that mentoring and executive coaching have grown in popularity in the business world. People learn from others who are more experienced in their field. I asked some successful business owners what hard-won advice they could give to aspiring entrepreneurs. Here's what they said:

"Everything always takes more money and more time than you think it will. Check out every opportunity and don't give up."

– Catherine Marshall, Executive Director,
  CAMEO, Oakland, CA

"Business is first and foremost about people, relationships, and community. Build lasting relationships by helping others build their business. When I join a business networking group, my goal is to help 20 other businesses grow. My experience has been that their businesses and mine have grown way beyond our expectations!"

– Jim Horan, One Page Business Plan Company,
  Berkeley, CA

"If I had to name one characteristic that is absent from most unsuccessful business people, it would be patience. I take a long-term view of my marketing activities and my business growth. I'm in it for the duration; it's the same way I approach financial investing. Patience will produce consistent results and steady growth. One final thought would be to spend less time pursuing dollars and more time pursuing relationships. Business success is about relationships – and relationships take time."

– Jeff Rubin, Put It In Writing, Pinole, CA

"Solo piloting your entrepreneurial flight requires you to be committed to self-monitoring. Initially, when your blank date book is only full of potential, launch yourself by reciting daily affirmations. Dress as though you have a full day of appointments. Then, design and activate a detailed workday schedule with specific objectives. This infrastructure will sustain you as you move forward and transform your goals into achievements. You will soar on your new found wings to amazing heights!"

— Margi Urquhart, Realtor, Alpharetta, GA

"My advice is Listen! Advice and support comes from many different sources. Don't let your ego get in the way of listening and hearing what may possibly be the best advice in the world."

— Sady Hayashida, Hayashida Architects, Emeryville, CA

"Start out on the right foot by keeping good records. Accurate record keeping is an essential element in measuring the success of your business. Opening a separate business account for all business-related earnings and expense transactions will enable you to track your spending habits and budget your expenses. It is also a useful tool in planning a marketing strategy. Tracking your income stream allows you to better recognize seasonal earning trends."

— Diane Tyler, D. L. Tyler & Associates, Oakland, CA

"I'm always amazed at how many business owners don't follow up with their customers on a regular basis. I've built my travel business by delivering what I promise, following up, and going that extra mile for customers."

— Barbara Gordon, author,
  Are You Switched On!, Berkeley, CA

"I've been in private practice as a psychotherapist since 1990. When I started, I had no safety net financially, and I was both frightened and exhilarated. But I was fulfilling my dream. Most importantly, I just kept stretching myself to keep taking one step at a time until my dream became real. Within 6 months, I had a full practice, and it has been full ever since, with 20-25 appointments weekly. Two things really helped me: I joined an established practice with a solid reputation and referral base, and I was willing to relocate to an area much less saturated with practitioners than the nearby San Francisco Bay Area."

— John Colladay, psychotherapist, Antioch, CA

"Make sure you are IN LOVE with what you do in your business life, because how you earn your paycheck affects your personal one. Compromising a few ideals when you first start out is not a crime. However, it's important to understand where to draw the line and set goals to not repeat mistakes made or lessons learned as a result of doing so. If everything comes easily to you, then, where's the challenge to grow? This is as true for a successful business as it is in life."

— Alicia Brite, color consultant,
   The Color Effect, Berkeley, CA

———————

Recently, I received an e-mail that contained a list of ways to enjoy life. They also apply to entrepreneuring:

"Open your mind to new ideas; create adventures, uncover your talents, and believe in magic."

— Anonymous

PART FIVE:

Market and Sell Your Socks Off!

Chapter 26:

Mind Your P's and Q's

As a kid, my Mom used to tell me to "mind my P's and Q's." I never quite knew what the P's and the Q's meant, but I knew they were important in getting along with others and being successful. I've noticed that people who have been in business for awhile mention remarkably similar characteristics that have helped them keep their business and enthusiasm high. Here then, is a list of P's and Q's that you may consider minding to help maintain and grow your business.

> *Most importantly, be patient with yourself; you can't do it all, or all at once!*

P's

Planning

Planning is essential. For example, write a marketing plan and update it regularly. However, planning is what most people put off. They say, "I'll get to that. Right now, I have my plan in my head." Poor planning is one of the most common reasons for business failure, so take the time to write your objectives, make a plan to meet them, and follow through daily, weekly, and monthly. Track what worked and what didn't, and revise accordingly. Follow the trends that affect your business on a regular basis, and make changes as needed. Pat yourself on the back when business is rolling in; but keep your eye on the future and plan for it. *Careful and consistent planning works.*

Persistence

Remember the story of the tortoise and the hare? Who won the race? Keep going. Keep connecting with carefully targeted customers, following up on leads, producing excellent service, and developing ongoing business referrals. However, sometimes you don't need to do anything except listen to your customers and continue giving them what they want. In time, your efforts will pay off, just as the tortoise won the race. People want to do business with people they can count on to do the job and who will still be in business in ten years.

Patience

Be like a cat that is after a mouse. Wait until the time is right and then pounce – on opportunities, that is, not customers. You will want to push your business growth curve, and you may get impatient with slow results. However, try to do what you can control; then, play the waiting game. Put your marketing plan in motion. If advertising is part of your marketing mix, run your ad for at least 3 months. Don't pull it too soon. Potential customers may have seen your advertisement nine times and just decided to call you. But then, when they look for your advertisement the next time and it isn't there, they will call someone else. You never know for sure when your prospective customers will sign up for your service or buy your product. Most importantly, be patient with yourself; you can't do it all, or all at once!

Q's

Quotas

Sales professionals have sales quotas. So should you. Figure out what you need to make this year in order to turn a profit. Set sales benchmarks for your company. Break down your projected sales for the year into monthly sales quotas. Keep track of the sources that produce the most income. Adjust your work to focus more time and effort on those sources in order to build business and increase cash flow. Make time for those activities that may not generate immediate income but will generate ongoing business. Developing and maintaining your own professional network will keep you up to date on market trends, produce referrals, and create valuable business connections.

Quality

When was the last time you experienced excellent customer service? Quality is easily recognized, but can be a challenge to produce. Too often, companies extol their superior customer service, but don't follow through. If you consistently provide excellent service, your business will thrive. People will drive miles to do business with you. Customers want products that work, service that gives them value, and responsive, polite, effective customer service when problems arise. If a customer is unhappy with your service, resolve it; don't give him a laundry list of excuses. We're a service-oriented economy. Your type of business can be duplicated by many others. You will stand out by delivering quality service and being responsive to your customers.

Quiet

Allow yourself free time to do those things you like but think you can't because you have too much to do for your business. Your business will improve if you take quiet time for yourself. Of course, this doesn't mean that you have to meditate. Your quiet time could be the simple pleasure of reading a good book or walking on a beach. Whatever gives you a sense of peace and quiet, build it into your weekly schedule. Some business owners say that taking regular vacations helps their business grow. Why do you think that is so? It allows you time to relax, and gives you a new perspective on handling your business with renewed energy.

Chapter 27:

Why Market Research?

Remember the movie, "Field of Dreams?" – "Build it and they will come." Many first-time owners simply open the doors of their business and expect that customers will rush in to buy their new widget or service. On rare occasions, this is exactly what happens. However, for most new businesses, it takes careful planning and positioning to bring in customers and keep them. A business will not succeed just because you are enthusiastic about your product and you want to succeed. This will provide the motivation to build your business, but the business must be built on careful initial and ongoing planning.

Is There a Market?

The first step is to determine whether there actually is a market for your products or services. This process is called *market research*. Analyzing your market and competition will help you decide whether or not to open your business doors. However, before you do extensive and expensive market research, ask yourself and other people in your field these questions:

- How many competitors provide the same service or product?

- If your product or service is innovative (i.e., not already known to the public), can you educate your market and create a demand for it?

- Can you compete effectively in price, quality, and delivery?

- Can you price your product or service to achieve a profit?

Researching the Market

If you feel satisfied that you do have a viable idea, move to the next step of researching your market in the areas of target customers, competitors, and industry trends.

- **Target customers:** Who are they? Where are they? How many are there? Is your service essential in their day-to-day activity? What are their needs and resources? Can they afford your products?

- **Competitors:** Who are they? How many are there? Where are they? How is their business similar or different from yours? What are their pricing strategies; value-added services?

- **Industry trends:** What is declining or growing in the industry as a whole or locally? What's happening in the general economy that might affect the buying trends of your customers? Is the industry seasonal?

This research effort pays off in increased profit potential, because you gain solid data that helps you to:

- Find out if there is enough demand for your product or service.

- Determine the promotional mix that's most likely to reach your target customers.

- Develop critical short- and mid-term goals.

- Identify and prepare for market changes.

"Why Will Customers Buy from Me?"
– Defining Your Market Niche

After your market research is complete, it's time to ask yourself the question: "Why will customers buy from me?" The answer is your competitive advantage. You must determine this before you promote your business. When you define your market niche clearly, you will spend your time, money, and effort in satisfying those customers who value your niche – for example, you may want your business to be the women's clothing boutique that features the latest fashions from New York or Paris. Spend your time and dollars on becoming known for what differentiates your business from your competition.

Market research is essential to help you develop your niche. A market niche does not just happen. It is carefully thought out and planned. Yet once you clearly have a market niche, the right customers find your door and will come again and again.

If you have read this far and are thinking of starting a business, you may be thinking, "This is a lot of work. Can't I just make my best guess and see how it goes?" Yes, you can. Just remember that well over 50% of businesses fail in the first 5 years of business. And one of the biggest reasons is poor planning. If you do your market research at the beginning and track market changes on a regular basis (every 6 months to a year, depending on your industry), yours will be one of the businesses that SUCCEED.

A Quick and Easy Competition Study
To help you better position your business, check out your competition. Remember: Your competitors can include educators, friends, and foes. All types can provide useful information. You simply use different techniques to gather information, depending on the type of competition. Talk to your competitors, ask questions, do informational interviews with those who are willing, act like a customer yourself, or send a mystery shopper.

Choose at least two of the following elements, and compare how your business or business idea deals with them in contrast to how at least two of your competitors deal with them.

1. Pricing

2. Delivery

3. Hours available

4. Location

5. Promotion

6. Quality

7. Web presence

8. Selection of services

9. "Value-added" offerings

10. _____

MY BUSINESS	COMPETITOR 1	COMPETITOR 2
_____	_____	_____
_____	_____	_____
_____	_____	_____
_____	_____	_____
_____	_____	_____
_____	_____	_____
_____	_____	_____
_____	_____	_____

Chapter 28:

5 Secrets of Marketing Your Business

At the end of the year, look back over what you have accomplished in your business and ask yourself: "What made my business successful? What marketing techniques brought in the best results? What flopped? What do I need to do differently or better next year?"

When you're redoing your marketing plan for the next year, keep these five "secrets" in mind:

1. **Write and work your marketing plan.** A plan does no good collecting dust on a shelf. Implement and measure each marketing activity. See what works and what doesn't. Make appropriate changes based on client response.

2. **Be visible as an expert in your field.** Speak at professional organizations, conferences, and clubs. Write articles for industry newsletters, local newspapers, and magazines. Start your own e-newsletter or write a book.

3. **Follow up.** Always do what you promise and, when possible, do more than is expected. You will create loyal customers and great word-of-mouth referrals.

4. **Choose marketing techniques appropriate for your target market(s) and use them consistently.** One mistake entrepreneurs make is using techniques with which they are comfortable, but which don't effectively reach their market.

5. **Build, maintain, and nurture a network of contacts and colleagues.** Don't be a lone wolf. Few business owners have built their business without help.

Secret number 5, a network of contacts and colleagues, is the most important for building a successful business, especially for sole proprietors. It is a source of support, guidance, strategic alliances, and marketing ideas, as well as referrals. Consider some of these practical marketing tips from "in-the-trenches" independent business owners:

Practical Marketing Tips

"Visibility is very important for my business. I host a table at local Job Fairs. After awhile, people recognize me and feel comfortable that I am reliable and consistent. When I join clubs or associations, I always dress professionally and often ask women I meet to model for me. This is particularly effective, because most of the women are flattered, and they offer to host a presentation."

— Arleen Alfonso, Weekenders Clothing

"If you have a website, spending 10 minutes a day online promoting your site can have an enormous impact. You can find other websites to exchange links with, search engines to post on, and online communities to join."

— Julia Stege, GraphicGirlz.com

"Keep a tickler file for phone calls. Tally contacts made on a calendar sheet so you can see what you're actually doing each day and track contacts-to-business booked. This way you know how many phone calls, pieces of mail, etc. you need to make to get 'x' amount of business."

— Ronelle Coburn, Life Purpose Analyst

"Seek opportunities to collaborate and to educate. Work with others who are in related fields and create events that educate broadly – adding value to people's lives in aspects beyond one's own particular business. As independent business owners, it's great to come together, learn from each other, inspire, and be inspired."

– Maggie Ostara, Clarity Breathwork™ Practitioner

"When you follow up with a client who's asked for information via email, end your message with a one-sentence inspirational message and signature tag. When cold calling, don't hang up when you get voicemail. Have your focused message ready and leave your name and number at the beginning and end of the message."

– Melissa Mischak, Tsirigo's Orbit

"Use a contact database as a technical solution to ensure that you capture details about your contacts that offer you an edge. For example, wouldn't it be nice to know when you last contacted a business and who you spoke to and what you spoke about?"

– Bryce Forney, CPA,
  Forney Accountancy Corporation

"Don't sacrifice sales while doing your marketing. Marketing just supports sales. If you think of it as building relationships or solving other people's problems, suddenly you've taken that negative connotation out of it. Small business is about building relationships, understanding what people want and making sure you or your product are a good fit for their needs. It is important to listen to what your market wants from you, what they'll pay, and what they want changed about your product in order to buy it!"

– Allison Bliss, Allison Bliss Consulting

CHAPTER 29:

10 Simple Ways to Get Referrals

Have you ever heard a consultant proudly say, "I get all my business through referrals"? Have you ever wondered how they accomplished that? Why is referral business so coveted? Because "word of mouth" saves you time and money. Generally speaking, most people want to do business with people they know, like, and trust. If you ask a friend for a referral, you trust their judgment and try out their recommendation. You, as the consultant, also get a pre-qualified lead for your business – a person who most likely fits the criteria for your ideal client or customer. You haven't spent any advertising dollars, and the client is more ready and willing to buy your product or try out your service.

Generally speaking, most people want to do business with people they know, like, and trust.

Perhaps you are saying to yourself, "I've heard this before. I know I should be marketing my business more, but I can't seem to get started." So here are 10 simple ways to create referrals:

1. **Tell 6 to 10 people about your business each week.** Don't leave your office without your business cards and your 30-second answer to the question, "What do you do?"

2. **Project a consistent image of your company** in all promotional materials – business cards, letterhead, postcards, website, newsletters, advertisements.

3. **Be client-driven:** Meet their needs. The number-one way to find out what clients want is to ask – and then listen. Respond by acknowledging their request and developing a solution. Then deliver consistently and on time.

4. **In initial customer contacts, be welcoming and willing to answer questions or concerns.** On voicemail, leave an informative message and let clients know when they can reach you and when you'll get back to them; then, follow through. Good first impressions are crucial.

5. **Consider a double-sided business card.** Put a menu of services and products on the flipside. It serves as a mini brochure.

6. **Keep a calendar of your marketing activities for each month.** Attend at least 2 activities per month, even when you're busy! This keeps potential customers in the pipeline. Revise your calendar according to what type of marketing activities work the best for your business. Add more of the activities that work, and drop the ones that don't.

7. **Join and participate actively in your local Chamber of Commerce** and appropriate professional organizations and community groups. Remember, people do business with people they know and like.

8. **Practice the art of conversation** – listening and sharing, and getting to know more about your customer or potential client. Conversation is a give-and-take proposition, like a dance. Be friendly, humorous, engaging, and not just focused on doing business. People will appreciate you and your interest in them.

9. **Walk your talk.** How can you advise people to do what you yourself are not doing? Do what you advise others to do, and make sure you deliver.

10. **Set aside time every day to do one marketing activity** – even if it's a 5-minute telephone call. This will constantly keep you connected with your current and potential customers. People can't do business with you if they don't know who you are or what you have to offer.

And a bonus tip:

11. Add to this list. Choose just one idea and use it consistently for a month.

The #1 Key to successful marketing is to choose a set of simple and effective marketing activities that match your strategic plan, and do them consistently.

The #2 Key is to choose those activities that best fit your target market(s), rather than what is easy for you to do. Most importantly, remember that the most carefully detailed marketing plan on paper won't work unless you make it real by putting it into action.

CHAPTER 30:

Sales Tips to Help You Sell with Confidence

Your business plan is done. Your office is in order. Your business cards, brochure, website, and ads are ready. You even have a list of qualified leads. There's only one thing left to do, and it scares you silly – sell! How can you take the scariness out of sales? Turn those customers into friendly folks who need solutions to very real problems. Think of yourself as a problem buster.

Most people have too many daily hassles to deal with, so you can make doing business with you a bright spot in their day.

Tip #1: Listen

Your potential customers want something. That's why they're calling you in the first place. It does little good to tell them about all your services when they may only be interested in one. Find out what that is by asking questions and listening to the answers. If you have a service that you truly think will help this customer, explain it to them. Ask if they have any questions or need further information or clarification. Often, your customer may simply appreciate that you listened to them. If they don't buy then, they'll remember you, and either buy later or refer your service to others. Don't forget to follow up with them at regular intervals.

Tip # 2: Share

Think of selling as sharing information, resources, and helpful suggestions. The personal touch of calling, rather than sending written information by fax, email, or snail mail, makes a big difference. Smile, call customers by name, and avoid being pushy. Deliver your product on time, and follow up. When people decide to buy something, they usually feel a sense of urgency. Make sure you do what you promised as well as delivering a quality product or service. This builds trust and return business.

Tip # 3: Qualify Your Customers

You can follow the first two tips to the letter, but if you're talking to people who don't want or can't afford your product, you're wasting your efforts. For example, no matter how wonderful your cold-water taffy is, a person with dentures won't bite. Make sure you are reaching the appropriate target market for your business.

Tip # 4: Offer Solutions

Match your service or product to the customer's needs. If there is not an exact match, you may actually offer the best-fitting solution, which customers can try on their own, and then say, "If that doesn't work out for you, call me and I'll be happy to help you." Also, don't talk about the features of your product or service before the customer has bought into its benefits.

Tip #5: Build Relationships

Be visible in your community. Participate in trade, professional, and social organizations. Most national professional organizations have chapters in major cities. Offer to give a talk at one of these organizations in your area. They are always looking for good speakers. You are not the only salesperson for your company; customers who like what you have to offer will refer their friends to you. People want to do business with people they know. It has been shown that satisfied customers tell 3 people about the product or service they liked. If you have 50 actual customers, this means you have 150 potential customers. Be the merchant in your community who's known for friendly, reliable service, or the consultant who is happy to refer a colleague if her expertise doesn't fit a customer's needs.

There are many ways to make life easier for your customers, such as answering their requests promptly, solving a problem the same day, taking the time to chat, or offering free delivery. Most people have too many daily hassles to deal with, so you can make doing business with you a bright spot in their day.

CHAPTER 31:

Why You are Always Selling a Solution

No matter what business you are in, you are selling something. Why will people buy from you? It's because you have something they want, or they have something to gain by doing business with you. People want to buy solutions to problems. No matter what you sell, you have competitors.

So what compels people to choose you? Two things: uniqueness and benefits.

So what compels people to choose you? Two things: uniqueness and benefits.

Uniqueness

What makes your business unique? Determine your business's uniqueness by asking *yourself* questions such as:

- "What do customers praise most when they e-mail, write, or talk to us?"

- "How do employees, customers, suppliers, and friends describe what we do?"

- "What do we offer that our competitors can't?"

- "What problems do our product or service solve?"

- "If my mother-in-law were buying a service like ours, what would she look for?"

Then ask *your customers* questions like these:

- "How would you describe our product to your friends?"

- "What would you say to recommend our service?"

- "What made you choose our service?"

- "What do we do that you haven't found at other similar companies?"

- "How can we improve our service or product line?"

- "Why do you visit our store/place of business often?"

As you compile and ponder this information and do some on-going market research, it will become clearer to you what makes your business unique. Position your marketing to deliver that message – a message that answers the customer's basic question, "What's in it for me?" Get very specific so that people who hear or read about what you offer will know what problem you will solve and the benefits of doing business with you.

When you have decided what makes your business unique, make up a catchy slogan of four to nine words that paints a picture of your business. For example, an accountant might say, "We do numbers right!" Be creative; add a dash of humor. Describe in a few words what makes you different from your competitors in terms of size, customer-service policies, employees, mission, speed, cost, or time. This "picture" of your business makes it easy for current customers to refer you to others.

Benefits
Whatever you are selling, benefits are what your customers are buying. What benefits do your customers get from you? Business owners often make the mistake of selling *features* rather than *benefits*. In a market where many companies sell similar products or services, the customer wants to know what benefits you offer.

For example, when you buy a car you know that all cars will provide you with transportation. However, you select a particular car because of its benefits, such as one that fits your budget, your climate, and your self-image. Here are a few more examples of the difference between selling features and benefits:

Feature: 24-hour grocery store.
Benefit: It allows you to buy food at your convenience.

Feature: Airbags.
Benefit: It protects you and passengers in case of an accident.

Feature: Accounting services.
Benefit: It helps you sleep better, knowing that your books balance.

Which benefits are *your* customers buying? Often the most direct way to find out is simply to ask them. You may think you are offering certain benefits, but do your customers think so, too? Find out by giving them a simple questionnaire and asking them:

1. List what you like about our product or service.

2. What is the single most important reason you buy our product or service?

3. What convinced you to buy our product or service instead of a competing one?

Then ask these same questions of your best customers and continue asking "What else?" until you uncover the real reason they keep coming back. Build your business around that.

Remember: Since others have similar products/services to yours, your primary product is actually how well and how consistently you reward a customer's confidence in you.

To grow your business, know what makes you unique and what customers perceive as the benefits of doing business with you. And keep delivering those benefits.

Chapter 32:

Exercise: "Why Should I Buy from You?"

The 4 P's of Marketing

The 4 P's of marketing are *Product, Place, Price,* and *Promotion.* Once you have determined your target market(s), you want these potential customers to know about your product or service and why they should buy from you. Marketing is all the activities you initiate to secure your position within the market, or the total possibilities for generating revenues for your product or service. When you have determined who your target market is and your slice of the total market, it's time to craft your positioning statement – a statement that answers the question:

"Why should I buy from you?"

The Importance of the Positioning Statement

Your positioning statement shows how you are different from your competitors; it differentiates your business and emphasizes your uniqueness. A well-crafted statement is a very effective SALES TOOL! It is a concise, powerful statement that, when delivered genuinely, will go a long way towards closing a sale. It can also be used to introduce yourself at networking events. It is often called "The 30-Second Elevator Speech," because that is about as much time as someone will listen to you before they start asking questions or move on to the next person. You want to pique their interest, so they want to find out more about how you might help their business.

The positioning statement has three components:

1. Your company and/or your name.

2. A statement about how your product/service addresses the problem/need, as identified by your target customer.

3. Your key point of differentiation (your niche).

Here are some ways to differentiate your business:

- An impressive list of clients.

- A solid customer-service track record.

- A unique approach that delivers better results.

- Added value to your product or service.

- A focus on specific deliverables in quality, service, or price.

- A specific target market.

Example of a 30-Second Elevator Speech
Hi, I'm Dana Arkinzadeh and my business is DMA Organizing. I am a professional organizer of homes and businesses in Alameda County(California). Interested in improving your health? Clear out your clutter and get organized! Don't lose a contract because you couldn't assemble the information needed to do a proposal! Disorganization causes stress and stress can directly affect your health. Improve your health by letting a professional organizer take the stress out of getting organized! Go from clutter to clarity with DMA Organizing.

Try It!

My company and my name are: _____

_____

I/We work with (*target customers*): _____

_____

who are (*state problem or need here*) _____

_____

Our product/service is: _____

_____ ,

which provides (*key benefit*) _____

_____

What differentiates my service/product (*your niche*)

in the marketplace is: _____

_____

_____ .

Chapter 33:

Strategic Networking

The basic networking process is a highly successful marketing strategy for getting you into companies before they actually formally begin looking for a consultant to help them solve a problem. If you happen to show up just when they're thinking they need someone who can do what you offer, your sales process is shortened, and you may be able to sign a contract very quickly. Why? Because (1) you don't have to compete with other consultants, (2) you have a great opportunity to show how your skills can benefit them and provide solutions for their immediate needs, and (3) most companies prefer to hire consultants they know, or who are referred to them by trusted colleagues, friends, and employees.

Networking Tips
- Networking is a valuable skill for many business purposes. Build relationships with your network contacts. Everyone networks, especially when looking for new business or consultants.

- A key building block is a well-prepared 2-minute introduction or presentation that clearly and succinctly gets across what you have to offer. Customize your introduction to fit your prospect.

- Pursue leads systematically to obtain more meetings.

- Good follow-up is as important as good meetings. You will get results if you keep following up with your contacts. You will also stand out from the pack. It's amazing how many business people don't return phone calls or e-mails, or follow up with what they promised.

- Networking definitely leads to business meetings. Well-conducted informal meetings produce door-opening referrals, as well as insight into a particular company's needs and culture.

Here Is a System to Help You Make Networking Pay Off:

1. *Research your target company(s).* Find out as much as possible about the company's culture, products, services, changes, or problems faced, as well as the names of key contacts.

2. *Talk to friends and colleagues to find a contact within the company* with whom you might be able to meet before you send the approach letter to the key contact.

3. *Develop an approach letter.* Your goal is a meeting with the key contact. Use a referral name, if you have one – it improves your chance of getting a meeting dramatically. In the letter, include some information that you gleaned from your research, and include a day and time when you will call.

4. *Develop a 15-second phone script* and follow up the letter with a call at the time you stated. Request a time for an informal meeting.

5. *After you schedule a meeting, plan what you want to cover in the meeting.* The meeting outline can include:

   A brief presentation: Your 2-minute introduction, which captures your experience and strengths and illustrates specifically how you might be able to work together.

   Main discussion: Be prepared with 2 or 3 questions about the company's issues. Keep discussion conversational; acknowledge the other person's ideas, ask follow-up questions.

Generate referrals: especially if there doesn't seem to be a match between the company's needs and your services. Ask for a specific type of referral.

Handling referrals: Ask questions such as: "Why does she come to mind?" "How do you happen to know him?" "In what areas do you think she could be helpful or especially interested in my expertise?" Answers to these questions help you write a better approach letter or make a more effective phone call to the referral. Also, ask if you should call the referral yourself or if the person making the referral would prefer to make the call on your behalf.

Ending the meeting: Stick to your time agreement. Take the initiative to end the meeting. If appropriate, ask what the next step would be to move forward with a consulting project. If the person is willing to talk longer, she or he will indicate interest. Express your thanks.

6. *Debrief yourself directly after the meeting.* Write notes so that you remember the information; jot down questions and everything that the person told you about the company.

7. *Follow up the meeting with a thank-you letter or e-mail,* whichever is appropriate.

8. *Follow up with each referral,* using the same procedure.

9. *Create a system for keeping track of each referral meeting date,* connections, important information gained, and results of each referral meeting.

10. *Follow leads and possible projects or contracts* as far as you can with the target company(ies).

Remember that contacts made and relationships built will lead to consulting projects coming your way. If your initial contact doesn't pan out and you still want to work with a company, keep in touch – it may result in work when you least expect it!

Chapter 34:

Customer Service as a Sales Tool

Several years ago, a sales representative told me a story that I've never forgotten. He attended a motivational sales training program at his company. After the speaker gave a talk to about 100 employees, he approached the CEO of the company and said, "I can pick out your top three producers from this audience."

The CEO, intrigued, said, "Okay, show me who they are."

The speaker pointed to three individuals in the audience.

Amazed, the CEO asked, "How did you know? Those three people are consistent producers, even in down times."

Listening, professionalism, and your unique way of adding value to your service create customer loyalty.

"Easy," the man said "While I was giving my talk, I looked out at the audience. The three people I picked were obviously engaged and listening to me. But beyond that, I felt an intangible feeling of connection with them – call it interest or enthusiasm. They caught my eye and I felt heard. Your customers feel the same way, and buy from them."

What does this story have to do with delivering quality customer service? Everything. Building a relationship with your customers grows your business. Listening, professionalism, and your unique way of adding value to your service create customer loyalty.

Here are four ways for small business owners to deliver excellent customer service:

1. *Cultivate the quality of listening demonstrated in the story.* Customers are not shy about telling you what they want. Listen, ask questions, and then deliver what they want to the best of your ability. For example, a small bookstore may take a few days longer to receive a book you ordered; but if the owner knows what you like to read, he may make helpful recommendations. As a result, you are more likely to order from him, especially if he calls or sends you a postcard when new books arrive that fit your taste.

2. *Be responsive.* How many times have you called a business and been put on hold for five minutes or told that you need to speak to someone else who will call you right back and never does? A few simple ways to stand out among your competitors is:

   - Return calls promptly.

   - Fax information the same day it is requested.

   - Place an order immediately.

   - Get a written proposal in *before* the deadline.

   - Have a friendly, detailed, helpful message on your voicemail.

   - Answer calls in person or hire a receptionist.

   - Refer customers to another professional if you don't offer what the customer wants.

   - Do what you promise and be willing to handle problems as they arise.

3. *Get to know your customers beyond the scope of business.* Be generous with your time, especially when dealing with new customers or clients. Make them feel welcome and comfortable. Build a friendly relationship. Be personable, warm, and genuinely interested in them. For example, my family has gone to the same dentist for years. His office hours and location aren't very convenient, but we all love going to him because he tells jokes and remembers to ask something about each one of us. How many people go to the dentist and get to laugh?

4. *Try to handle the dissatisfied customer diplomatically.* Dissatisfied customers are apt to tell more people what they *disliked* about your service than satisfied customers will tell about what they *liked*. For example, I bought an outfit from a small boutique, but after getting it home, I decided I didn't like it. The next day, I took it back to the store and asked if I could exchange it or get store credit. Since it was on sale, the clerk told me that she would not take it back – "All sales are final," she said, as she pointed to a tiny sign behind the counter that I hadn't seen the day before. It would have been so easy for her to offer store credit or an even exchange. I would have been happy with that and remembered next time that all sales items were final. Instead, she lost a customer, I kept the outfit I hated, and told at least 7 of my friends about the incident.

Now, every business owner has encountered not just dissatisfied, but truly difficult and demanding, customers. What do you do? I have found that taking a detached professional attitude can diffuse a difficult situation and complete the transaction with a minimum of personal upset. In these cases, it is appropriate to be less personable and more efficient.

In short, as a small business owner, you can assure your customers feel served, and know they can count on you to deliver. Remember, it is much easier to keep a customer than to generate a new one. Being in business means working with all types of people, and successful business people are those who master the art of being appropriate to the situation, are sincere, and are accountable.

CHAPTER 35:

How to Warm Up to Cold Calls

Marketing and sales are the lifeblood of any business. Marketing means everything you do to secure your position within your market segment. Your market includes the total possibilities for generating revenues for your products and services.

Discover a sales style that suits you. A key to sales success is to choose your strategy and put it into action consistently.

What, then, is sales? Simply put, sales is bringing in the business – the revenue that produces the profit for your company. Every business owner has their own style of making sales. However, at some point as a business owner, you will face making cold calls.

When I ask my clients what scares them the most about starting their own business, many say "Selling myself," or "I hate making cold calls." Even people who are already in business often say that they like talking to their friends, current clients, and colleagues about their business and enjoy working on their projects once they make a deal, but they dread making cold calls.

Here are some practical tips gleaned from my experience and those of my clients and colleagues for making cold calls work for you:

1. *Make each cold call a warm call.* The easiest way is to use a contact name and say, "Mary Smith suggested I call you." If you don't have a referral, write a letter with a special offer. Follow up your letter with a call and make reference to your letter. Always do your research on the contact company. Use information gleaned from your

research to establish a connection when you call. Talk about an issue facing their company, and focus on their needs.

2. *Choose a time of day when you are most energetic to make your calls.* Plan the number of calls for that day, take a deep breath, sit up straight, and do them all at once. This creates a momentum. One suggestion made to a colleague of mine makes sense: make 5 calls each day. You feel nervous before the first call, you feel better after the second call, you feel confident after the third call, you feel great after the fourth call, and you feel successful after the fifth call. This is regardless of the outcome of each call, because you reached your goal of 5 calls a day. The calls will get easier each day, and you will get results.

3. *Write a script for your calls.* You may want to write one script for voicemail and another script for talking live. There is a difference between the two, and you want to be prepared for both. The purpose of a script is to clarify what you want to say. Practice your script so that you can remember the points you want to make. You will change what you say to each person you talk to, but you will remember what you want to say and do it naturally.

4. *Stay organized with a contact-management system.* You can keep track of each contact and the result, as well as make notes about pertinent information and when and how to follow up. If you tell someone you will call them back on a certain day, you want to make sure that you call them back on that day, and with the information you promised. A system will help you remember.

5. *Be a problem solver.* People are looking for solutions to their problems. Don't push for a close on your first call. Ask for a meeting to explore their needs and how your service or business can provide them with solutions. Sell benefits, not features.

6. *Think about how you like to be "sold."* Develop your presentation around that. Be natural and conversational, and ask questions so that you can tailor what you have to offer to fit the customer's needs.

7. *Don't forget to smile.* Studies have shown that a smile travels across phone lines and creates a positive impression.

Discover a sales style that suits you. A key to sales success is to choose your strategy and put it into action consistently.

CHAPTER 36:

Dealing with Down Time in Your Business

For many businesses, the busiest time of the year is the holiday season. Yet for some entrepreneurs, that's the slowest time of the year. All businesses experience seasonal income ups and downs; but it can be feast or famine from late November until the end of December. In which category does your business fall? If your business is feasting, get your running shoes ready and prepare for the marathon. If your business is hungry, it may be time for creative belt-tightening. Here are 10 tips for taking control of your down time while creating business for the New Year.

10 Tips for Taking Control of Your Down Time

1. *Take stock of your products and services.* Be very specific as to what worked and what did not. Decide what to keep, improve, or delete. If you are a one-person business, this can be a difficult process. Think about hiring a consultant to assist you. You need to take an honest look at which of your services are in demand and which need some zip. As only one person, you must spend time on those services that have a high payoff. You may need to give up a pet project if there isn't a viable market for it.

2. *Get organized.* For example, budget time to update your customer mailing list; learn a new database or contact-management system that will improve access and maintenance, so that you can communicate quickly and easily with your customers.

3. *Attend a professional organization's holiday events.* If you only want to go to one such event, pick the group you've been meaning to attend but haven't as yet. You'll make new contacts and possibly gain new perspectives and ideas for your business.

4. *Reconnect with your professional and personal networks.* Update them on your business progress and new services. Explore how you might do some strategic partnering. After all, out of sight is out of mind. Your contacts won't refer business to you if they haven't heard from you in a year. Reminder: It's best to do this regularly throughout the year. Set aside time each week for networking. Write it in your calendar now.

5. *Write a newsletter.* Plan to mail it after January 2nd, so that your newsletter is one of the first pieces of mail your clients see when they return to work after the holidays. Plan to produce a monthly or quarterly newsletter. If this is too daunting, team up with another complementary business owner and produce a joint newsletter. Pick a theme for each newsletter and contribute information from your unique perspectives. Business owners I know who write a regular newsletter say that their volume of business increases significantly after each newsletter.

6. *Request testimonials from current and past customers.* Besides making you feel better about your business when business is slow, you will have testimonials on hand to share with prospective customers, to include in a new brochure, a newsletter, a proposal, and conference materials. An easy way to get your request returned is to include a form with one or two questions for your customers, asking what they liked about your service. Be sure to include a question about what they would like to see improved, as well. Include a line for them to sign to grant you permission to use their testimonial in your materials. Don't forget to include a self-addressed stamped envelope.

7. *Offer to do project work for other business owners* in your personal network who may be swamped during the holiday season. Or bid several projects with a deadline in November. This will bring in cash during your slow season.

8. *Review your business and marketing plans.* Revise as needed. Write your goals for next year. Then write the steps you need to take to reach those goals. Put benchmark dates in your calendar to check up on yourself. Do a specific, prioritized, action item list for January.

9. *Put balance in your life.* Spend more time with your family and friends. Do those leisure activities for which you haven't had time. Relax, and give yourself permission to enjoy your time off.

10. *Plan ahead for the slow season next year.* Project how you can meet your financial goals during the rest of the year. Take a well-earned vacation in December

PART SIX:

Making Room for More Business

CHAPTER 37:

How to Tickle Your Customers

Remember the tickler file – the original contact-management system? Use it or an electronic version to keep in touch with your customers, colleagues, vendors, and other referral sources. Whatever system you devise, however, you need to use it consistently. It's expensive to attract new clients, so you want to keep the ones you have. The 80-20 rule applies – 80% of your business comes from 20% of your customers. It pays to keep that 20% of your current customers happy.

Another thing to remember: One unhappy customer tells 7 or more people about the terrible service she got at XYZ Company; one happy customer tells 4 or fewer friends about the incredible service she got at ABC Company. Even though you have happy customers, they don't tell as many people about you as they would if they *didn't* like your product or service. How can a contact-management system tickle and delight your customers, so that they love doing business with you – *and tell their friends?*

Build a relationship with customers by:

- Being authentic and patient.

- Showing that you care.

- Being responsive.

- Not making excuses.

- Delivering what you said you would, and on time.

- Making it easy to do business with you.

- Going the extra mile and giving your customers respect and more than they expect.

Here are some suggestions for the care and feeding of your customers:

1. To keep in touch, all you need is a good database and contact-management system with all the "bells and whistles," which you update regularly.

2. Send thank-you notes for their business and referrals, and cards for their birthdays. Call with no agenda, just to see how they are doing. Set a goal of sending at least 3-5 thank-you cards per week.

3. Send an e-newsletter regularly, containing useful information and news about your company.

4. Have a customer-appreciation open house at your business, with an interesting program and food.

5. Greet customers by name when they come in or call. Talk about something they told you about earlier.

Remember this: Approximately 63% of customers leave because they felt ignored or were treated indifferently. If you follow the simple suggestions above, your customers will think of you first when they or their friends, colleagues, and family need your product or service!

CHAPTER 38:

Expanding Your Business

There comes a time in the life of your business when you need to expand to meet marketplace needs, opportunities, and/or personal goals. Here are a couple of ways to do this

1. *Create a partnership with a competitor, a new investor, or a talented colleague whose strengths complement yours.* You join together and create one business. For example, let's say there are two hat companies in the same city. One specializes in women's hats and one in men's. The marketplace favors one-stop shopping. You provide it together, as the XYZ Hat Company. Be sure to read up on the details of partnerships and write and sign a partnership agreement. (See Chapter 10.)

2. *Create a strategic alliance.* Say that you want to build your business but can't do it on your own, or you don't want to hire employees. Or perhaps a current client has asked you to do a project, and you don't have the expertise to handle a part of it – and you don't want to say "No." Instead of taking on unwanted new employees or recruiting a permanent partner, you can team up with another consultant or business to jointly market and deliver that particular product or service. Your businesses remain separate, but you subcontract with each other to deliver the service under one business entity. After the venture is complete, you and your strategic partner may decide to continue working together on the same product/service, or to create a new project that fits both of your businesses. For example, a marketing consultant and a CPA might form a strategic alliance to offer a start-up package that includes a marketing plan, financial projections, and

coaching to people who want to start a small business or grow their existing business. Of course, you and your strategic partner may also decide not to continue working together, once the initial joint project is complete.

For both ways of partnering, be sure to draw up a written contract that all parties involved agree to and sign. Once you decide to work together, the following 7 principles will help ensure success and increased revenue for your business.

1. *Have an Idea that's Bigger than You Are.* Your vision for the expansion of your business needs to be greater than just you. It's obvious that you can't accomplish it alone. All partners need a shared vision, commitment to purpose, follow through, and teamwork.

2. *Be Honest about Your Personal Goals.* Understand each other's agendas and methods for building your joint business projects. It is also essential to be straight about how much time and money you will contribute to each project and to clearly identify how you will share profits and handle losses. It needs to be a win-win situation for all involved.

3. *Keep the Lines of Communication Open.* Include input from all partners, especially when making major decisions. In the case of strategic partnerships, it's crucial that everyone involved share clearly what each individual business culture needs. Each joint project needs a point person. This person will act as the decision-maker for daily operations.

4. *Have a Plan for Every Project.* Develop a joint business plan for each strategic project. Make sure that you lay it out carefully, measurable objective by measurable objective, step by step, with specific assignments for all involved – what I call "what by when and by whom."

5. *Do Customer-Focused Marketing.* You need to be focused on the customer, be nimble, and constantly assess the market so that your positioning is right. This is an ongoing process. You need to take a fresh look in order to adjust your offerings to meet your customers' needs.

6. *Be Alert to Problem Solving.* In every project, there will be bumps along the way. Do regular reality checks, revise your plans as necessary, and communicate when problems arise so you don't let misunderstandings fester. If your joint mission and commitment is great enough, good planning and communications will help you handle problems and keep on moving.

7. *Don't Forget to Celebrate.* When you achieve your project goals, celebrate your victory. Do something outrageous to acknowledge your hard work. Give crazy awards. Stop. Reflect. Savor.

Finally, don't forget to evaluate all aspects of the project, the partnership, and your business mission before you move on to the next phase of your business growth and partnership. Learning from the mistakes you made the first time around is essential for a dynamic, strong, and vibrant partnership.

CHAPTER 39:

Hire Wisely the First Time

Amy just landed a large project. She already has several projects going and five more in the pipeline. After celebrating her success, Amy realizes that there is more work than she, as one person, can handle. It's time for help. In the past, Amy has hired part-time contractors to help her, but now she consistently has enough projects and profits to consider hiring one employee. Amy is tempted to hire the part-time contractor she used on her last large project because it would be easy and quick. However, she knows that the contractor's skills aren't exactly what she needs for her new project, and she has doubts about the contractor's brusque manner with clients. Amy has never interviewed and hired an employee.

In your questions, emphasize what candidates have done in the past, because that is a good predictor of what they will be able to do when they work with you.

If you're like Amy, what can you do to get the best possible person for your growing business?

Ask yourself: What are the three personal qualities I would like most in an employee? It is a well-known fact that a large percentage of employees who get fired are fired not because they can't do the job, but because they can't get along with their co-workers, managers, or the customers. It is crucial to evaluate the candidates' professional qualifications and personal traits according to your criteria and your business needs. However, personal traits are the most difficult to evaluate accurately. Above all, you and your employee need to be a good match, not only because this suggests that the two of you will work together well but also because your employee's performance and ability to interact with your customers directly affects the success of your business.

How can you discover if a candidate is a good fit? One good way is to prepare interview questions that help you draw out information about his or her business knowledge, personal qualities, and "people skills." These questions tend to be more open-ended than simple "yes/no" questions, and to focus on how someone has handled specific situations in previous jobs.

Remember, your employee represents you and your company. Choose wisely.

For example, say that you want to hire a sales person. Once you have determined the person's sales skills, you will want to focus on how they would fit into your company's culture. You may like your sales people to be relaxed and casual, good listeners, relationship builders, and solid team players. Design your questions to help you get a sense of how good a listener or team player the applicant is. On the other hand, another business owner who is looking to hire a sales person may be seeking someone who is highly competitive, autonomous, and goal oriented. The sales person he chooses would not be a good match for your company.

Here are some sample questions to ask a prospective employee:

- "Tell me about a time when you dealt with an irate customer? How did you handle the situation, and what was the outcome?"

- "What project are you proud of? How did you contribute to the success of the project?"

- "Give an example of where you came up with a creative solution to a problem."

- "What motivates you the most?"

- "How would your last supervisor describe you?"

In your questions, emphasize what candidates have done in the past, because that is a good predictor of what they will be able to do when they work with you.

Interviewing Tips

- *Write a job description* that states your company's mission and what skills, traits, and qualities you require in an employee.

- *Request a cover letter* from the applicant so that you can get a sense of his or her communication style and personality.

- *Ask each candidate the same set of questions.* This makes it easier to determine the top candidates, because you're comparing apples to apples. In addition to assessing how well candidates answer the questions, listen to your intuition and pay attention to your gut feeling. Those feelings are usually quite accurate.

- *Conduct the initial screening via the telephone* to verify skill sets and get a sense of personal characteristics. Also, the voicemail message and the candidate's response time can be revealing. Invite for a face-to-face interview only those candidates who meet most of your criteria. This can be a real time-saver.

- *Be an astute listener.* It's hard to learn much about another person if you do most of the talking.

- *Try to make the candidate as comfortable as possible.* The candidate will be more forthcoming. Adversarial interviewing techniques to determine how well a person can act under pressure usually don't work.

- *Note how the candidate's car looks inside and out,* if possible. You may be a neatnik, while the candidate is a pack rat. Dissimilar organizational habits can create havoc in the office.

- *Check references thoroughly.*

Whether you're hiring your first employee or your fifteenth, it's crucial to find the person who's the best match for the job and for your company. A mismatch can cost you time, money, and business. It may take longer to find an employee who fits your criteria in the first place, but it's easier in the long run than trying to get incompatible people to work well together. Consider consulting a professional who is experienced in hiring to help you screen and recommend appropriate candidates, as well as help you hone your interviewing skills. It will be money well spent. Remember, your employee represents you and your company. Choose wisely.

Chapter 40:

Are You an Independent Contractor Or an Employee?

Many freelancers and consultants choose to work as independent contractors, and love working for a variety of companies on many different projects. However, it's important to know if you are really considered an independent contractor in the eyes of the IRS. Independent contractors are self-employed business people who are hired by a company to perform specific projects – for example delivering training programs, or fixing software applications as a computer specialist. Independent contractors are much like vendors, except that they perform intangible services rather than supplying goods.

The general rule of thumb is that a worker at a company is not an independent contractor if the company has the right to direct the person with respect to when, where, and how the project work is to be performed. If the company specifies only the desired results of the project, the person is usually considered an independent contractor.

There's a lot of room for interpretation in this arrangement. Even when the company does not exert control, if it appears that they have the right to control how a contractor completes a project, the contractor may be reclassified (by the IRS) as an employee. The reason the IRS is interested in reclassifying independent contractors is that an employer is required to withhold taxes from employees' pay, whereas the government depends on self-employed individuals to report their own taxable income.

There are at least 23 factors the IRS looks at to decide whether or not a worker is actually an independent contractor. The following is a list of the 13 most common factors. As an independent contractor, protect yourself by making sure at the beginning of a contract that you:

1. *Request a thorough, clearly stated contract with the company*, which includes (a) the specific results you are expected to achieve for a project and (b) that you, as the independent contractor, determine the ways and means of completing the project.

2. *Obtain specifications regarding the outcome of the project*, but don't ask for instructions from management.

3. *Accept no company-sponsored training program.* The IRS views this as "employee" development.

4. *Ask that the work duration be limited to a specific time period* for one or more specific projects. Include this in a written contract.

5. *Invoice the company on a project basis*, even if you are doing several projects for the same company.

6. *Require no set hours of work*, although you can specify approximate hours per week and completion deadlines.

7. *Specify your own place of work*, if possible, for the particular project.

8. *Pay your own expenses.*

9. *Do contract work for more than one company.*

10. *Show that you are a business* by having a business name, using your own business cards, and by being incorporated. (Note: Being a sole proprietor with a "DBA" may not be enough.)

11. *Work among the staff on-site*, but not as an integral part of a company project team.

12. *Voluntarily choose to provide oral or written progress reports with respect to meeting deadlines.* However, the company cannot require you to submit such reports.

13. *Make sure your contract agreement contains termination limitations* so that the company cannot terminate you "at will," as with employees.

These are useful guidelines. However, they do not replace a consultation with a competent attorney or tax advisor about your specific case. You can obtain further information from your local Employee Development Department (Form # DE38: "Employment Determination Guide"), and from the Internal Revenue Service, which offers guidance in IRS Publication 1976. Remember, it is in the company's best interest to follow the basic guidelines for independent contractors, because there are serious tax consequences to the company. The IRS always fines the company, not the contractor. However, it is also in your best interest to make sure you meet the qualifications as an independent contractor. The guidelines can be very confusing, so don't assume that your client company is up to speed on the regulations.

Chapter 41:

Retaining Good Employees

When you first opened your business, you might not have thought of yourself as a boss of anyone but yourself. Now you have two or more employees in your business. The question you might be asking yourself is, "How can I get my good people to stay?" When you hired your employees, you did everything you could to choose the best person for the position. Let's assume that you succeeded in hiring two outstanding people, and that they since have become an integral part of your business. At some point, one of your employees might get an offer to work for someone else. You cannot prevent that person from taking a great offer; but you *can* make your employee think twice before moving on.

> *One rule of thumb is that the cost of losing an employee equals between 6 and 18 months' salary; other hidden costs are lost sales and customers.*

In order to keep a valued employee, you may be tempted to find out what compensation he or she has been offered, then match it if possible. However, it's probably too late; you may have missed the boat a long time ago. The reality is that from the day the new employee walks in your door, you need to figure out how to keep him/her satisfied and productive. You may be thinking, "I don't have time to figure out exactly what will make my employees happy." Think again. The hiring process can be very time-consuming and costly. One rule of thumb is that the cost of losing an employee equals between 6 and 18 months' salary; other hidden costs are lost sales and customers. It is definitely worth your while to keep those people who are helping your business succeed.

> *They will feel ownership if their ideas, inspirations, and creative solutions are welcomed, encouraged, and incorporated into the company goals.*

Paying more money – compensation – is not the only way to keep good people. Although it is a very important factor, other things also factor into optimal work for an individual, such as: recognition for work well done; opportunities for professional growth and learning; rapport with colleagues; team work; casual dress; flexible work hours; and family-friendly policies. As a small business owner, it is essential to offer benefits that are intrinsically valuable to the individual employee because, unless you have venture capital funding, you can't compete with larger companies on salary and benefits.

Here are some simple yet powerful strategies to consider:

1. *Ask.* Simply ask your employee, "What would make you stay here? What might lure you away?" You may be afraid that they will ask for something that you aren't able to make happen. They might – but at least you will know what they want and have a greater chance of coming up with a way to meet that. If you ask and listen to what your employee has to say, he or she will probably be very surprised, and pleased that you care and respect her enough to ask.

2. *Include employees in setting organizational goals.* They will feel ownership if their ideas, inspirations, and creative solutions are welcomed, encouraged, and incorporated into the company goals. There will be things that employees complain about, but if they know their input is valued, it will more often be constructive criticism. People like it when their ideas are heard and considered. If the ideas are not implemented, that is usually okay – but the fact that you listened makes a big difference.

3. *Provide family-friendly policies.* What can you do that helps your employees keep a healthy balance between work and family? The easiest policy to implement is flexible work hours. You will probably get more and better work from employees who can come to work after dropping their kids off at school, or who can occasionally leave early to watch a child's soccer game or school play. Allow telecommuting one day a week, if possible. There are many ways to institute family-friendly policies. It's worth it in the long run.

4. *Promote collaboration and connection.* Make your work place somewhere you can tell a good joke, chat with coworkers, and bounce new ideas off each other. When people feel connected, they enjoy their work more. Ways to bring employees together informally include: hosting a breakfast once a week; sponsoring a lunch in a park in the spring; or giving them an afternoon off after a particularly great company accomplishment. Invite a speaker once a month to talk about a topic of interest to everyone. No one wants to be a lone wolf. If your business is a place where people feel free to be themselves and are appreciated for the work they do, they'll stay with you.

As you can see, these strategies don't cost much money, but they can make the difference between a valued employee leaving or staying with you.

Chapter 42:

Exercise: Action Plan – What's Next?

Now, it's your turn! Where does your business need improvement? What new service or product have you been thinking about providing? How can you take your business to the next level?

Use this action planning exercise to start making it happen – one step at a time.

Research the Market

My next step is: _____

_____

_____

Do Careful Financial Planning

My next step is: _____

_____

_____

Find a Viable Market Niche or a New Niche

My next step is: _____

_____

_____

Do a Business Plan (each year)

My next step is: _____

_____

_____

Develop and Maintain High-Quality Products and Services

My next step is: _____

_____

_____

Implement and improve a Customer-Service Plan

My next step is: _____

_____

_____

Develop, Revise, and Maintain a Consistent, On-Going Marketing Plan

My next step is: _____

_____

_____

Implement the Action Plan

My next step is: _____

_____

_____

Planning is essential – but nothing happens unless you IMPLEMENT your plan. Work your plan and watch your business thrive!

About Susan Urquhart-Brown

 This guidebook is the result of the author's 10-year journey of growing her business, learning what works – and what doesn't – for entrepreneurs, accidental or otherwise. This practical wisdom originally appeared in the column, "Going Solo," in the *San Francisco Chronicle* from 1998-2001. Urquhart-Brown updated and revised the information to bring readers a seamless and informative guidebook on entrepreneurship.

Susan Urquhart-Brown began as an "accidental entrepreneur" in 1993. Spurred by workplace issues, she began working with a career counselor. At one point in the process, Urquhart-Brown had an "Ah-ha!" moment. "I want to do what you do," she told her counselor. "I want to help people discover what they are passionate about, and choose careers that let them express that passion and expertise."

And thus was born the accidental entrepreneur. Urquhart-Brown says, "I never expected to end up as an entrepreneur. The term itself was the furthest thing from my mind. But what I did know was that my background as an educator, trainer, conference planner, non-profit program director, and courageous career changer made me ideally suited to help others find that missing ingredient in their career lives."

Finding her passion, Urquhart-Brown graduated from John F. Kennedy University in California with a degree in Career Development in 1995. Starting her business, she shortly realized that there was more – much, much more – to building a business and marketing than she realized. Urquhart-Brown has been intentionally building her business and, as a business coach and advisor, helping others do the same. Committed to helping clients and readers bridge the gap between where they are now in their business, and where they want to be (even if that bridge is foggy, unclear, or non-existent). She helps them build on their strengths, revise their business goals, and develop a plan to achieve their refocused goals. She specializes in coaching both newly minted and experienced "SoloPreneurs."

"I passionately believe that people should choose work that really suits them well. Many people start businesses that ultimately fail for a variety of reasons, but one reason is that the business was not a good fit for their personality, skills, interests, and what makes them tick! It takes tremendous drive and perseverance to run a business. I believe that it's essential to assess your entrepreneurial fit before you start a business. Once you get started, don't be a lone wolf. Don't mistake going Solo for doing everything yourself. The one secret successful entrepreneurs agree on is – ask for help when you need it!"

– Susan Urquhart-Brown, M.A.

For BOOK ORDER information
and the free quarterly e-newsletter,
EZ Steps,
please visit CAREER STEPS
at

www.careersteps123.com

For more information about
individual business coaching packages,
speaking, and workshops,
please contact
Susan Urquhart-Brown at:

www.careersteps123.com

or
Career Steps Consulting & Coaching
4112 Park Boulevard
Oakland, CA 94602
Phone: (510) 531-2071